SIND
A RE-INTERPRETATION OF THE UNHAPPY VALLEY

SIND
A RE-INTERPRETATION OF THE UNHAPPY VALLEY

BY

J. ABBOTT, I.C.S., B.A. (Oxon.)

PUBLISHED FOR THE UNIVERSITY OF BOMBAY

GYAN

Published by

GYAN

Gyan Publishing House
5, Ansari Road
Daryaganj, New Delhi-110002
Phone: 011-47034999, 9811692060
E-mail: books@gyanbooks.com

Distribution Network
gyanbooks.com
India, USA, Canada, UK, Australia, France

ISBN : 978-81-212-4017-8 (PB)
First Published, 1924

2nd Impression 2021

Printed at: Gyan Press, Delhi.

Sind
A Re-Interpretation of the Unhappy Valley
Author: J. Abbott

SIND

A RE-INTERPRETATION OF THE UNHAPPY VALLEY

BY

J. ABBOTT, I.C.S., B.A. (Oxon.)

PUBLISHED FOR THE UNIVERSITY OF BOMBAY

HUMPHREY MILFORD
OXFORD UNIVERSITY PRESS
LONDON NEW YORK TORONTO MELBOURNE
CAPE TOWN BOMBAY CALCUTTA MADRAS

1924

CORRIGENDA

pp. 46, 47, 53, 62, 64, 77 : *for* Mir Ma'asumi *read* Mir Ma'asum
p. 36, l. 27 : *after* Michelborne *delete* borne
p. 44, foot-note, l. 30 : *delete* result
p. 49, foot-note 2, l. 22 : *for* Unarand *read* Unar and
p. 64, foot-note 1, l. 2 : for *Jami'ul-Tawarikh*, read *Jami'ul-Tawarikh*

INTRODUCTION

SIND is unfortunate in its record. Inscriptions and archæological finds have hitherto added little to our knowledge of her past; her written record leaves centuries untold and buries the truths of other centuries in fiction. Her geographical features, by their apparent simplicity, have perverted research and added mystery to mystery unsolved, theory to theory irreconcilable; geographical factors have played a destructive part the extent of which we cannot gauge.

It is wellnigh impossible to write a continuous history of the valley. The interest of the valley, however, is probably in proportion to her many mysteries; the lure of exploration is always there to attract; her history and her geographical changes alike baffle interpretation, and the pursuit of an ever-elusive solution makes research into her past a perpetual adventure.

In consequence of the limitations of her *materia historica* one can write of Sind's many problems only with great diffidence, but the falsities that pass for fact are so crude, the fiction so bold that masquerades as truth, the conflicting theories of savants so numerous, that it is time to call a halt and review what measure of achievement has been made. I have attempted with this object, as far as I can, to verify every reference to native and European record that I have followed, and to leave a copy of the same for the reader to analyse for himself; I have examined the whole English record of the East India Company and European travellers, neglect of which alone is responsible for many errors, and in the form of essays I have attempted to cover the whole period of Sind's history.

Several of these essays have already appeared in issues of the *Calcutta Review*; many another essay is an enlargement of an article that has been printed in the *Pioneer*. I have pleasure in acknowledging the courtesy of the Editors of these papers in allowing me to use my earlier contributions.

Alibag, J. ABBOTT.
29th July, 1924.

CONTENTS

I

THE UNHAPPY VALLEY

THE UNHAPPY VALLEY

WHETHER notoriety is fame or fame notoriety, or, like fancy and imagination, these are masked words for the literary to unmask, I leave to you. I will use a word of no offence. The reputation of Sind is only too familiar as a valley burdened with all the plagues of Egypt, for an applied title of grimmest promise given to it by Burton has done more than any conquest or travel to draw the valley from its retirement into the range of general knowledge. As easy to remember as the lilt of a running song, it has crystallised in one unfortunate phrase, 'The Unhappy Valley', the impressions of half a century, and delivered them thus to subsequent years as a reasoned epitome of the valley's features. Its facile condensing of thought assumes, with the effrontery of epithets, the appearance of a permanent truth, and ensures that after seven decades of British occupation the popular idea of Sind remains an unexamined legacy from the early years of the last century. In specious clarity it is like 'The Silken East', and such familiar epithets of the East, that allow scope for the unguided imagination of the ill-informed and for the accretions of careless thinking.

A clever piece of journalism was the final coping to a structure slowly under erection since the beginning of the century, and the first visit of Pottinger to the courts of the Mirs. Concentration upon the misrule of the Mirs, an appreciation of the value of the *Pax Britannica* that we would now voice with subdued insistence, assisted in fostering this representation of Sind; but more potent factors than these were failure to appreciate the many causes, other than misrule and devastation, that have littered the valley with ruins, and a sentimental recalling of a past that was imperfectly understood. To the overwhelming impression of decay and departed glory that Pottinger, Postans, Kennedy and Burnes in total succeed in conveying, Burton added the light and shade of chiaroscuro.

It was in no small measure a fiction, this reputation of the nineteenth century, though based upon the sternest realism, for it had the elements of a romance constructed out of realism;

of a Utopia reversed by the same methods of selection and emphasis that builders of Utopias have always employed. By studied contrast and exaggerated conflict Burton instanced and picked out the evils of the valley only to glory in their number and strength, in much the same way as Kipling exults in the heat and loneliness of the exile's work in India. No enthusiasm for Sind was ever dimmed by a reading of *Sind Revisited*, and the lover of the valley, so far from having an issue to contend with Burton, welcomes him as a co-initiate, for one reads *The Unhappy Valley* and *Sind Revisited* as one reads *The City of Dreadful Night.* The evils are not so painted that we would not from sheer interest in new experience depart from our common road to share the sensations of the writer. Reading, we are compelled to think that evil is greater or less than it is painted, or, on the other hand, that the allure of evil is beyond resisting. Kipling has fashioned, with all the heightened colouring of stage scenery and its restricted semblance of truth, an India of half-truths as a background and stage for the spirit of the West. Burton has done much the same for Sind, though, whereas Kipling wrote in acknowledged fiction, Burton clothed and disguised his fiction in the garb of a traveller's record. And whereas the protagonist in the drama of Kipling is the spirit of a nation, in Burton the protagonist is self.

Now save that in the days of the Moghul Bakhar was a penal station for ministers who had incurred the imperial displeasure, there is nothing in any way a precedent for this depressing view of Sind. The Greek would have rejected with surprise a conception of the Indus valley which erred so far from seeing in it a Utopia that it beheld in it a purgatory. For he looked upon the valley with restricted vision. He knew of its rainless summer and again elsewhere of its monsoon, but he thought only of the parts about the river. He compared it with Egypt, he peopled it with mighty kingdoms where man lived beyond a century free from disease and the curse of too much law. It was to him a distinctly enviable land, and his idea of the Indus valley lingered long as an influence directing Western fantasy. Those ten months in which the Greeks dropped down the Indus can be traced in the long held view of

India as a country cultivated by the beneficent overflow of rivers, and blessed with a climate more equable than was to be found in the West.

To the Arab, likewise, the valley was no unpleasant spot. He knew Mekran and its dried-up valleys, and by the deserts he had invaded Sind. The advance guards of his invading armies had seen the valley from the low passes of the Kirthar hills as an arid, sterile and stony plain with bad water, and, like Solomon,[1] depressed by a similar view of the higher Indus plains, had turned away in disgust from an oppressive land. But when he had conquered the valley he knew it for what it was, and his descriptions, running on clearly marked lines, present a picture of desert and pleasant oasis. He was quick to notice the absence or presence of trees, and in particular of the palm, and he was still quicker to note the quality of the water. Mansura, where neither grape nor apple nor walnut grows. Kandail, where the palm tree does not grow. Nirun, where trees are rare; and Debal, not over-abundant in large trees or the date palm. And the oases of Sind. Sadustan, remarkable for the number of its fountains and canals; Manhabari, in a hollow of pleasant aspect with gardens and fountains and running waters; Kalari and Alor, pretty towns upon the Mihran and Samand, where water is obtained from wells. Only the Arab, perhaps, would thus think of Sind as a collection of shady oases, for he had reached the valley through the wilds of Seistan, Mekran and Baluchistan, and, like the Israelite, learned the weariness of heat that gathers in barren hills and passed through the immensity of desert light to gain a promised land.

Still later comes the view of European travellers and English merchants, in the seventeenth and eighteenth centuries. To these again Sind was a coveted land; a fruitful and pleasant country, rich and fertile almost as covetousness could wish, for they saw little but the precincts of Tatha in its prime. The gradual decay of Tatha, indeed, is at least one explanation of the contrast between the European view of Sind two and three

[1] Tradition relates that King Solomon ascended the Takht-i-Suleiman to view the plains of India and turned away from conquest in dismay at the aridity thereof. The first projected Arab invasion of Sind was abandoned as a result of the depressing account of the desert given by the advance guards of the Caliph.

centuries ago and that which usually prevails to-day. Burton would hardly have coined his catchword if he had seen Tatha in its spacious days. Camoens spoke of that 'most fertile region, Ulcinde'; his translator gave to it a new name, and notoriety instead of fame.

A last thought, and that a dismaying one, is that the modern readjustment of the economic centres and the commercial routes of the valley goes far to perpetuate the traditions of Burton's age. The desert of Sibi, at one time a plain of plenty, has now become one of the portals of Sind; westward, too, Karachi has taken the place of Debal as the port of the valley, and her most powerful impressions on the new arrival are those of utter waste and loneliness. Historically a portion of Mekran and not of Sind, she is accepted generally as the interpreter of the secrets of the valley, though she is divorced from the river and its canals and so from everything that makes Sind and inspires its charm.

Travellers' tales are like the sayings of the blind men who attempted to describe an elephant. Any one tale is apt in half-truth to conceal and pervert the truth. Sind, even more than India, has suffered from the blindness of travel. The Greek saw little more than the river and the parts it overflowed in season, and so found a Utopia in the valley. The early Europeans to reach the valley, in the seventeenth and eighteenth centuries, in turn saw little further than the precincts of Tatha, many went no further than her ports upon the sea, and so Sind became again a coveted land. To-day she is judged by the desert which shields her around from hasty approach—by the oldest of her wastes, that stretches from Karachi to the river, and by her northern and eastern deserts, with their hidden secrets of a fertile past, and it would seem almost as if she had thrown off some of the chains of confinement only to fetter herself more firmly with an ill-earned name. The Arab, and he alone, has seen her fairly, and this because he judged her not by her approaches; judged her not by the desert which had struck him with dismay; nor judged her by Debal upon the sea.

II

THE CLIMATE AND PHYSICAL FEATURES OF SIND

THE CLIMATE OF SIND AND PHYSICAL FEATURES

The Hills

Sind is a valley of many silences, and these proclaim the limits in which its restricted life-flow wanders. Silence of the desert and the immensity of light without shade; silence as of drowsy forenoon of those peaceful stretches of the river that have no allurement for the fisher; silence more solemn of the dreary wastes where the river joins the sea on a lonely and uninviting coast; but it has no silence so profound as the silence of its hills. For the desert has its nomads and its shrines—be they but seldom tended—the paths of men cross it and the fields of men adjoin it; the delta has its dwellers who love its level solitude with an ancient love, and far-faring boats drop down upon the flood from one busy centre to another through the recurrent silences of the river; but the hills have no share in the labours of the valley and the sound of human industry never reaches them to break their impenetrable stillness.

The Kirthar hills stand back from the kingdom of the river and its conquest of the desert, remote and indifferent spectators of the great struggle, themselves conveying with the attraction of their isolation a sinister impression of absolute uselessness. For the most part devoid of life and unadorned with the simplest ornament of nature, they have none or few of the multitudinous interests that add charm to small things; they must be viewed largely as a world rejected, a world in its first stage of accomplished birth, or, to use a familiar phrase, as little less than a lunar world dead and lifeless. In this way they are impressive by their mere mass, by the weariness of their constant repetition, and by their unchanging monotony. At times, where their dimensions are small, appearing like a newly-abandoned quarry, unnatural and repulsive in its exposure of creative secrets; and at times, in the width of their light-swept spaces, across which the weary eye can take no measure, uncanny in their perverted values of sound and vision. The sun of the desert beats on their barren sides and the heat gathers in their hollows, and it would be a vain thing to call them beautiful. Yet they are beautiful with the beauty of a crude impression, the coarseness and disorder of which dissolves in distance, for the distant prospect of their band of ever-changing colour, luminously pink at early dawn, deepening blue against the blaze of a cold-weather sunset, or delicate as the shades of silken gauze through the haze of heat, goes far to make one forget that the desert of Sind rarely shows the features of the desert of romance. So, in their own way, they are just as interesting as that great river which glimmers from their heights as a pale streak of light through the canopy of dust that always hangs over the valley. And they have been too long neglected not to have acquired something further from the glamour of mystery that attaches to all things long forgotten. Beyond them and beneath them is the borderland of the Baluch, its hills dotted with his simple expressions of a simple faith, and peopled with the thousand and one fancies that his imagination attributes to high places and the lonely edges of exalted altitudes; but the gods of the Sindhi are in the plains and the religion of the valley does not touch his hills. Their *ziarats* are few and but little more than local names; the translated souls and the dancing children of the border haunt not their slopes, and folk-lore draws from them no inspiration. The Sindhi has no Khalifat and no Chiltan. And it was even so from the beginning. The burnt and blistered defile of Hinglaj shelters a pilgrim resort long famous in the East, old as the days of Chaldæa and older far than the religions that now send there their trains of devotees, and the dust-grey hills of Las Bela are hollow with the temple-caves of Buddha, but the Kirthar never had their gods. Barren as hills seldom are save in the desert, their wall-like front rises abruptly from the levels below with little assistance of foot-hills to break the gradients of their ascent, demanding attention except when hidden by the veil of summer dust, and yet the man of the valley knows nothing of them even in proverb, and their restricted life leaves them to an exclusion more complete than that of any other natural object they behold.

This very exclusion of the Kirthar hills from the life of the valley is so complete, though its sun-drenched valleys are marked by many a relic of former irrigation,[1] as to suggest that in yet one more way the history of Sind has been allied rather to that of Asia beyond than to that of the Indian peninsula. One is tempted to regard them not so much as a boundary to the valley as a proscenium behind which lies the great arena of ancient civilisation more antique than that of Greece, the great stage on which in tragic fashion has been played the drama of nature, and the history of world migration and the rise and fall of nations has been written in the varied rainfall of centuries. One is tempted to accept their barrenness as a tidemark of a wave of dessication which has engulfed the greater part of the ancient world.

The Delta

Of the similes that deltas afford—of how they show a river fretfully embracing every hope to escape the oblivion that awaits it in the sea, or of how, as a few only have dared to say, in them the toiling river nears the fruition of its desire—of all this one might write much. This much, at least, may be written, that a delta appeals strongly to those imaginations that love to find the thoughts of sentient things in the inanimate objects of nature. And if you be one who draws from this manner of coming to an end a simile of despair—and you will have many a well-known name in literature to aid you—the delta of the Indus should give you confidence in your choice, for a more dispiriting scene it would be hard to imagine.

There is first the belt of desert, which curves along the edge of permanent cultivation and behind the desolate levels of the coast. And on the fringe of this desert you may follow still, in the position of old ports, creations of the eighteenth century, the lie of an ancient coast. In the desert you will find, if you choose to wander there, scattered groves of dead trees, skeletons blackened and empurpled with long exposure, and

[1] These relics of terrace irrigation, *gohar-basla*, often of great size, are attributed by the Muhammadan Sindhis to infidels. They point also to shells that are found in numbers and call them the teeth of infidel giants. Occupation of the hills by the Hindus may have followed upon persecution in the plains at the hands of the Muhammadan conquerors of the valley.

crowning plots of raised ground, or a forgotten mosque or tomb isolated in a waste that stretches to its vague horizon with a monotony made more intense from place to place by that moribund aspect of decay which expanses of salt earth alone can convey. But the desolation of the desert has its limitations, and its loneliness is always somewhat melodramatic in its picturesque insignia.

It is a different matter when the desert has been crossed by waterway or desert path, and the empty flats are reached which form the restless outposts of this lone land. The desolation then becomes a scene of mordant shabbiness, where even the intricate network of waterways is dark with the wreckage of earth. Nor is its appearance less sinister where heightened banks permit of spasmodic cultivation; for the fairest aspect of the delta is only a study of the catastrophe, which, with the sea and swollen river, crosses and recrosses each year these levels to the furthest limits of the zone of desert, where the rayat erects his unstable dykes to keep out the infiltering flood.

It has its seasons. In the cold season its drab monotones are broken by patches of vivid colour, where the wild fowl find an unmolested sanctuary; oases of tawny gold and snowy white, where the brahminy and sheldrake, the pelican and ibis settle in their thousands, and the unbroken sky of day blushes with maiden blush as countless flamingoes rise in fleecy clouds of sunset rose. And as the night approaches, the mystery which lingers over these flats by day draws increase from the intangible secrets of a hectic and ephemeral beauty, when the damp and treacherous waste becomes one huge prismatic mirror, in which the splendour of sunset and afterglow is reflected in wondrous wise. And then the manifold cries of the birds, as they restlessly seek a resting-place for the night, add to the disturbing allure of unexpected beauty, the impression of indescribable loneliness. In the waning light of day the delta is the loneliest spot in Sind. It is still without grandeur of form and its beauty never loses the semblance of a mask, but for one brief hour it is a romantic portal of fairyland, inviting the Ulysses of every age to put to a test their adventurous hopes.

But if it is only in the cold season that the delta loses for a moment its repulsive ugliness, it is not till that season is over that it becomes an object without parallel in the valley. The isolated fields of the cold months are then covered by the flood of a river made more tidal by the force of the monsoon, and more destructive by the salt poison of the sea; the banks of the regular channels are then known only to the initiate, and from the doubtful security of artificial mounds the lingerers in this formless tract look out upon a horizon of water. The water-fowl have flown away; the cattle, which outnumbered far the entire population of the scattered hamlets, have been driven away on their long trek to the hills; the nomads of the desert have gone north or southward over the border; the desert shrines are untended, and the few human beings who remain live like marsh-dwellers in a world all but isolated from the rest of Sind. And on the bounds of this world the old ports see again the waters gather, and in their dull glitter a mocking vision of the past. It is not hard to understand why the mazes of the delta gave to the Sind coast for centuries the infamy of piracy or preserve to this day an atmosphere of suspicion.

The Climate

The monsoon is of such permanent interest to every part of India save the valley of the Indus, and of such persistent influence in directing the home wanderings of the exiled Anglo-Indian, that it is hard to imagine, within the regions of fact, an India without its south-west monsoon. And yet that one exception to the unity of the peninsula, the Indus valley, is responsible for the slow recognition of the annual work of the monsoon in the Western conception of the East. From a part framing a whole, the Persian, and after him the Greek, modelled an India in harmony with the attributes of provinces little Indian in their general features. They pictured an India of great desert and mighty rivers, but the monsoon they forgot, and this, though the heavy rains fanned into rebellion the grumbling of Alexander's army and the violence of the monsoon detained in the harbours of the Indus the river-built fleet of Nearchus.

India was a land of equable climate and regular seasons; upon the barrier wall of the northern mountain boundary the year's rain fell in abundance, and great rivers, finding thereon their source, worked downward and honeycombed the plains with their meanderings. Until the sixteenth century even books of travel—travel of wandering merchants, peregrinations of mediæval bishops, imaginative travel of stay-at-home monks—make comparatively little allusion to the monsoon on land, and much allusion to the rivers[1] of the continent, which legend made to flow with honey, oil and pellucid wine. The framework of mediæval record of travel in India, its petrified imaginings and accepted conventions, its limited power of observation and its slavery to hearsay, its broken descriptions and perverted proportions, carried on a memorising of a great tradition, and is therefore of unexpected value as a guide to the climate of Sind in classic days.

Simple, however, as the climatic features of Sind seem to-day, and approximate to those of the valley in the days of the Greeks, the usual solution offered of the many changes in the valley, that of a river constantly changing its bed, provides indeed no explanation of much that is puzzling in Sind history. Throughout that history, from the invasion of the Greeks up to the very eve of the British annexation, there runs a series of incidents evidencing changes that a westering river alone will not explain; incidents, in fact, requiring the introduction of

[1] The rivers of the Indians 'flow not with water, but one river with pellucid wine, another with honey and another with oil. The rivers flow for one month for the king, and this is his tribute, but for the rest of the year they flow for the people. So then they pass each day in the society of their wives at the sources and by the streams of the rivers, playing and laughing as if at a festival. Along the river banks flourishes in great vigour and luxuriance the lotus—they convey water in ducts . . . they have besides water-baths of two kinds, that which is hot and clearer than silver and the other dark blue by reason of its depth and clearness. In these the women and children swim about together . . . all of them models of beauty. Emerging from the bath I can fancy them lying down in the meadows, commingling their sweet voices in mirth and song, and there the meadows are of ideal loveliness and decked by nature with flowers and with trees. . . . Of birds again there is a great plenty, which make the hills resound with their songs. The wind, too, blows gently, and there is always an equable temperature, and besides all this the sky is there clearer than yours and surpasses it in the multitude and splendour of its stars. Their span of life is not less than forty years, and for all this time they are in the bloom of youth, and they know neither old age nor disease, nor want. . . . You must needs then acknowledge that the people of India are more blest than yourselves . . .' (*vide* Dion Chrysostom).

another source of change, perhaps even more potent than a changing river.

From time to time, for instance, the river would seem to have been of proportions far less than at present. The Greek historians represent the Greek campaign as proceeding despite all changes of season, and the transport of elephants from one side of the river to the other as a regular incident, even in the months that are to-day marked by a swollen river kept within prescribed limits only by studied art and a perfect network of dykes. Similarly, the Arab record shows no modification of campaigns by the season of flood, and this though the struggle of conquest was largely fought out in the delta. On the other hand, later accounts, from the sixteenth century onwards, show as an invariable custom of warring armies the retirement from combat in the middle of the Abkalani.

And then there is again the great campagna of desolation that forms the portal of Sind on every side, that separates the cultivated centre of the valley from the hills and runs like silent backwaters of the sea in and out of the valley, carrying memories of the dead to the very doors of the living. A changing Indus will not explain the creation of the desert between Jacobabad and Sibi, across which Krateros, with the heavy transport of the Greek army, marched without hindrance, and which in the sixteenth century was a plain of garden cultivation,[1] but which between the descent of Shah Beg Khan Arghun upon Sind and the accession of the emperor Akbar had become a prey to the simoon. From that time forth this northern frontier of Sind has borne a reputation as formidable as any desert of story, and the belief still survives that its hot winds, in the absence of protection, first slay and then completely dissolve the bodies of the slain.

[1] In 1514 a thousand camels were taken in loot from the gardens of the Kach plain (vide *Tarkhan-nama*). In A.D. 1588 Mir Ma'asum writes of an army going from Bakhar to Siwi and dying of thirst.

'In the plain of Siwi there were formerly many forts and much cultivation, but all is now waste: the hot wind blows there' (*Tarikh-i-Ma'asumi*).

'Between Siwi and Bakhar is a vast desert over which for three months of the hot season the simoon blows' (*Ain-i-Akbari*, vol. ii).

Cf. the *Memoirs* of Jauhar. Describing the retreat of the emperor Humayun from Sind, he describes the simoon to be met in season before reaching Mustung. He writes, 'In the hot season the simoon blows with such violence that the very limbs of a man are melted. . . .'

Nor will any caprice of the Indus explain the disappearance of those rivers that Arab record shows as joining the Hakra from the hills of the Kohistan, the remains of irrigation in the Kirthar range, or the ruins that mark forgotten highroads across the Kohistan plains. And then, lastly, there is the evidence as to a changing rainfall. Bernier wrote of the years when rain did not fall in the delta; Hamilton found that for three years rain had not fallen at Tatha, this in 1799; Westmacott wrote that for twenty years the rains of Sind had failed, and that the rayats complained of impoverishment following upon expense in binding for irrigation a river of reduced volume. Fond tradition to-day relates that the British brought back the rains. Still more there are a few examples of heavy rainfall recorded where now the rainfall is practically nil; legends of Uchch relate the rising of the river in the rainy season and the threatened destruction of the town averted by the brick of Khwajah Khizr, whilst in 1398 the rains of Multan were so heavy that the army of Amir Timur, which lay there under his grandson, lost all its horses.[1]

An answer to many of the questions that this perplexing and detached evidence, both of a change in rainfall and in the volume of the Indus, provokes, is perhaps to be found rather outside the limits of Sind than within its bounds, for it is obvious that the sources of the valley's water supply are amid the frigid silences of glaciers beyond the Himalayas, and that the rainfall of the valley plays no part in affecting the supply of

[1] 'At the same time intelligence arrived from my prosperous son, Pir Muhammad Jahangir, and the other nobles besieging Multan, who had been six months in the siege of Multan . . . now the rainy season had by this time set in, and the rain kept continually falling in torrents, so that most of the horses of my own stable and those of great numbers of the nobles and soldiery died, and we were obliged, by the heavy rains, to shift our quarters from our camp into the city. When some time had elapsed in this manner and scarcely a horse remained among us, the neighbouring zamindars and chieftains who had entered the house of subjection . . . when they saw our apparent distress all withdrew their feet from the highway of obedience. . . . Now since the nobles and the soldiers of Prince Pir Muhammad had lost all their horse during the rains. . . . I gave orders to my master of horse to produce 30,000 chargers, which I presented to Prince Pir Muhammad, thus furnishing his whole army with a remount' (*Malfuzat-i-Timuri*, an autobiographical memoir of Timur, translated into Persian by Abu Talib Husaini and dedicated to the emperor Shah Jahan).

'As the soldiers of the prince had lost their horses in the rainy season and had been reduced to ride on bullocks and to walk, the emperor presented them with 30,000 horses' (*Zafarnama* of Sharaf-ud-din Yazdi, died 1446).

the river in comparison with the rainfall of countries beyond. If parallel were possible between the changes in the climate of Kashmir and changes in the recorded variations in the volume of the Indus and rainfall of Sind, correlation of isolated examples of change might be easy.[1] From the sixth to the eighth centuries a dry epoch of Kashmir corresponds with the apparently depleted volume of the Indus at the time of the Arab invasion, and it is in this period that is usually placed the diversion of the river described in the legend of Alor. In the middle ages Kashmir was isolated by its excessive cold and heavy snowfall; it is at the end of this period that the northern parts of the Punjab (1334 *circa*) were swept by a flood that added for years another desert to that province, and about this same time appear instances of heavy rainfall at Multan. From the close of the Middle Ages returns a dry period in Kashmir, and in this the gardens of Kach become and remain a desert.

Such a parallel can be but sketched, but it forces conjecture that Sind has been saved from the fate of dessication that has swept over so much of central Asia only by the chance that its great rivers drew their bounty from the glaciers of the Himalayas.

[1] *Vide The Pulse of Asia*, Prof. Elsworth Huntington.

III

THE INDUS

THE INDUS

FROM old tradition, that it flowed due south from north, to the age-long idea that it entered the sea in the Gulf of Cambay;[1] from its legendary inclusion in the rivers that watered Eden to its mythical merging in a circumambient sea; from the days of Skylax and Nearchus, when to descend its stream was to approach the mystery of an incomprehended vastness, to the last adventure of Burnes, who with the spirit of the past travelled ahead of his baggage in impatient fret to view the classic stream; from days when in legend its source was in the Euphrates or the Nile,[2] to the time when Tod, in picturesque and swollen untruth, pictured it a thread of blue water meandering

[1] 'This celebrated river was once supposed to have flowed in nearly a direct south line from its source into the ocean' (Pottinger).

'In almost all the mapps which hitherto I have seen the river Indus is always described falling into the Sea at the inmost recess of the Gulph of Cambaia; which is a grievous error and as wide from truth as the whole Country of Guzerat is broad (and is no narrow one), for Indus, which is discharged into the sea with two very large mouths sufficiently distant, runs not on the East of Guzerat, as it should do if it entered into the sea by the Gulph of Cambaia, but rather on the West, and so far from the Gulph of Cambaia that all Guzerat, and perhaps some other countries, lye between' (Pietro Della Valle, 1623).

'I have one observation more to make of the falsenesse of our maps, both of Mercator and all others, and their ignorance in this country. First, the famous river Indus doth not emptie himselfe into the Sea at Cambaya as his chiefe mouth, but at Sinde. My reason is: Lahor stands upon Indus, from whence to Sinde it is navigable, to Cambaya not so' (Thos. Roe to Lord Carew, 1615).

Idem to the East India Co., 24 Nov., 1615.

'I will observe that the famous river Indus doth not poure himself into the sea by the Bay of Cambaya, but far westward at Sindu. For . . . it is navigable to Syndu; to Cambaya not, but certayne bye-streams begotten by the seasons of rayne make mightie inundations, which have cherished the error' (*Idem* to Lord Bishop of Canterbury, 29 Jan., 1615).

Vide also Sir Thos. Herbert: 'Not many leagues from Surat and near the Cambayan gulf is Diu . . . at the entrance into the Persian Gulf . . . confined by Gedrosia . . . a stream or arm of the Indus encompasses her so that she becomes a peninsula.'

'The next maritime Country to Sindy is Guzerat. The Indus makes it an island by a branch that runs into the sea at the City of Cambaya' (*A New Account of the East Indies*, Capt. A. Hamilton).

Vide also the Second Borgian map drawn up by Diego Ribero in 1529, to illustrate the partition of the newly-discovered regions of the world between Spain and Portugal. The Indus therein is made to flow direct south to its junction with the sea in the Gulf of Cambay.

[2] Duarte Barbosa says the Indus proceeds from the Euphrates. Al Masudi and Alberuni both correct the belief represented by Al Jahiz that the Indus flowed from the Nile.

along a hinterland of desert; even from these to the present hour, when its life course ends upon a lone, forgotten coast in a scene of moribund decay, the great river of Sind has had a chequered way.

Sanctified by many a hoary legend of miraculous power, here at Uchch stayed in its advance by the brick of Khwaja Khizr more effectively than any chair of Canute stopped the incoming tide; here at Alor, to save a threatened maid, drawn with its burden of ships from out of one course into another; identified again with Sarasvati, the purifier of celestial origin; withal its title Darya Shah,[1] the title of a king. Its old courses marked with many a name of village and town, its present going almost throughout the valley, a passing from silence into silence until it reaches oblivion in the sea; its course ever westering, its delta ever extending, its path strewn with the litter and ruin of abandoned cities whose lineage is beyond all tracing. The capitals of old were its associates; far-famed emporia the companions of its advancing delta—Patala, Bahmanabad, Alor, Mansura, Tatha the first; Barbarei, Debal, Lahribandar among the second; of these not one with a lifeline clear. And the delta, with its memories of the wild hopes of Alexander, reminiscences of Tatha in its prime and the spacious days of the Moghuls; a land of adventure to Persian, Greek and Briton alike, now lies divorced from the life of the valley, the measure of which is Karachi, alien in spirit, alien in origin from its deltaic predecessors as capital or port. To-day there is something anomalous in the apparent sovereignty of the King River, as it flows through the heart of the valley in neglect, its sole bond of continuity with its past its name.

The enthusiasm of a Western idealism for the reputed memorials of ancient Greece has touched wellnigh with sacramental touch the name of Sind's great river, and thrown over the history of the Indus a veil that conceals its realities. In the unexamined continuity of its name has been found assurance that the river's actual course has always been much as it is, and to such assumed permanence of direction Sind owes a mass of historical errors written with the gravest

[1] The Sindhi speaks of the river as *darya shah*.

sincerity in contemplation of a great idea. To the influence of an abiding name Sind owes the sweet unreason and poetic insobriety of the Alexandrian tradition, that has given to the chief settlements of to-day a legacy from Greece that they will surrender henceforth with reluctance; and to the reverence for the glory that was Greece and to its great control it owes the failure to recognise an historic inheritance from the Persian.

To Greece[1] is usually credited a modification of the Sanskrit 'Sindhu', that has given a name to a river, and to a peninsular continent; it is forgotten that the name Indus was really taken from the Persians by the Greeks, and by them passed on to the Romans, who gave it with fresh sanction to the Western world; that Indus in fine is not a Hellenisation of Sindhu, but a Persian title denuded of its aspirate.

It remains true, none the less, that though in origin an Oriental name, it is because the Greeks took it to themselves that it maintained in European use its supremacy over many another transliteration of local names. Whilst the Hindu persisted in calling the river Sindhu, whilst the Muhammadan historian and geographer spoke of the river of Sind and its affluents as the Mihran, the Ab-i-Sind, Aba-Sind or Nil Ab, and whilst again the Chinese,[2] in obvious imitation, spoke of the Sinto'u and Mila'n, the European, when after the break with

[1] *Vide* Raverty, 'The Mihran of Sind' (*J. R. Asiatic Soc.*, Bengal, 1892, p. 156, n. 3): '. . . the name Indus was and is unknown to Oriental geographers and historians. It was Europeanised . . . by the Greeks out of Sindhu, or they may have called it the Indus, as being the river separating Hind from Iran-i-Zamin . . . and not intending it to be understood that Indus was the proper name of the river.'

Tod thought Sindhu a purely Tartar or Scythic name.

Cf. Max Muller, *India*. Sindhu probably meant originally the divider, from 'sidh', to keep off. Even the Greeks called it Indos, the people Indoi, hearing first of India through the Persians. The neighbouring tribes, who spoke Iranic languages, all pronounced, like the Persians, the 's' as an 'h'. Sindhu became Hindu (Hidhu). And as H's were dropped even at that early time, Hindu became Indu. Cf. Pliny, 'Indus incolis Sindus appellatus.'

Now 'the Sanskrit . . . is Sindhu, not Hindu, from which the word Indus has come. . . . It is the ancient Iranians, the followers of the creed of Zoroaster, who first spoke of the river as Hindu and called the country as Hapta-Hindu. . . . India, the Western or the European name of the country, was first taken up by the Greeks from the Iranians, who called it Hindu.' The old Hebrew word for India is Hoddu. The Hebrew form Hoddu is said to be contracted from Hondu, another form of Hindu, the Avestaic name of the Indus or the Sindhu (*J. Bom. Br. Royal Asiatic Soc.*, 1916-17, vol. xxiv, No. 3, Art. xvi).

[2] *Vide* Hirt Rockill, *Chau-Ju-Kua*. Itinerary of Kia Tan, compiled A.D. 785-805.

classic days his interest was again turned East, followed the example of the Greek. And this example came then to him with a greater appeal, as it came with the sanction of the great Ptolemy, whose ideas survived long with many an anachronism.

Yet if the name Indus with its double sanction has prevailed, it has not done so without some conflict with names that are feeble transliterations of the Hindu and Muhammadan equivalents. The 'Sindu' of Cosmas, of Sir Thomas Roe, Thomas Kerridge and Fryer, and the 'Sindus' so common a feature of the reports of the East India Company's servants, seem transliterations of the Hindu name. 'Sind', 'Sindy', 'Sindeh', 'Sinde', that are equally generally used as names for the Indus even up to Rennell's Memoir of A.D. 1793, are more probably due to elision of the Persian *izafat* from the title Ab-i-Sind, in a manner similar to its omission in translations[1] of the last century. Whether modifications, however, of the Hindu or of the Muhammadan titles, such names are the usual rendering in the seventeenth and eighteenth centuries of the name of Sind's river, and the title Indus is almost a literary memory, save in this transformed way. Rennell's Memoir emphasises the distinction between these names and that of Indus by giving the former as names generally adopted by 'Asiatics' in contrast with that adopted by Europeans, thus enforcing a separation in origin of nomenclature that does not really exist. When the Greeks followed the Persians in the Indus valley, even as they accepted from them the Brahmanical wonder tales of mythology, so they took an Oriental title of the river; when the Europeans of the seventeenth and eighteenth centuries again descended upon the valley they accepted, in a similar way, the Oriental titles that they found in use, and in their own way attempted to copy them. And the promise of these centuries was considerable that the Persian name for the river would be lost in the names deduced from the current Hindu and Muhammadan titles.[2]

[1] Cf. the translations of Elliott and Lee, in which Ab-i-Sind becomes 'the river Sind' or 'the Sinde.' Van Linschoten remarks that the 'Portingals have given the river the name of the land.'

[2] The earliest instructions given by the East India Company for the exploration of the Indus delta (A.D. 1610) refer to the river Sindus or Saree; the record of the first voyage made to Sind by the Company's agents in 1613 alludes to the river Zinde.

The survival of the name Indus is, in fact, a facile illustration of the strength of literary tradition. Whilst the reports of the Company's factors, presidents and agents almost invariably contain modifications of the names still used in their time by the Hindu and Muhammadan, there is a tendency for the traveller more independently to retain the title Indus. In the seventeenth century there is, side by side with a mass of record that threatens to perpetuate a new title for the river, and one more closely resembling Sindhu or Ab-i-Sind than does the word Indus, a mass of literature that retains in classical imitation the use not merely of Indus, but of other one-time stock of the geographer. The influence of Ptolemy after the Renaissance militates against change, and preserves a title which might otherwise have been lost.

With the nineteenth century opens the last chapter in the history of the name Indus. The passing of Sind under the control of the British was in academic wise a reconquest of the valley by the Greeks, and in the face of the unbridled enthusiasm for the tradition of Greece in Asia that characterised the nineteenth century, the title hallowed by the Greeks received yet another sanction which promises to be its last. Out of the many Oriental names of the river, the Greeks transmitted to the Romans one that the Persians, conquerors of the Indus valley, had given it; this the authority of the great Ptolemy preserved in centuries when other Oriental titles had an influence more direct, and a militant enthusiasm, that had more faith than logic, revived in the nineteenth century its insidious appeal. Coloured almost from its beginning by its connection with Alexander, and its origin forgotten, it was a literary axiom to regard it as a naming by the Greeks, as something, in short, European in contrast to the confusion of Eastern titles; and in the belief that it was a European name Europe took it in the last century.

In the history of a name there are chance moments that forecast its future greatness, and even the retirement and self-immolation of Sind have been impotent to prevent the spread of the name of its river to two hemispheres. Parochial as is its record, secluded as the valley has remained for centuries from the larger history of the peninsula, its river has yet given its name to India, and its detachment is preserved in the 'Indies' of the East and of the West. From the naming of the Indus valley 'India' by the Iranians to the similar naming of the whole peninsula is but a sequence of time; to the chance that the first Arab invasions reached little beyond the limits of the valley is due the contrast of 'Sind' and 'Hind', that remained a literary distinction long after its *raison d'être* had ceased to be. The tradition that made the Indus a boundary between Irania and Hind; that made it again to the Greeks one of the natural boundaries of India; that occasioned the Arab separation of Sind and Hind; and made the Indus the bound of one of the three Indias of Nicolo de Conti[1]—in this in part is the origin of the multiple Indias that have left a memory in the 'Indies' of to-day.

A confusion of Africa with India is as old as the Romans. It reveals itself in the India Minor of Matthew Paris, in the Middle India of Marco Polo and Benjamin of Tudela, in the India Tertia of Jordanus, and in the never-ending controversy of centuries as to the location in mid-Asia or Abyssinia of Presbyter John, the half-mythical Oriental ruler of Christians. Our 'Indies' of to-day are reminiscent of this ancient confusion, but they are even more reminiscent of an actual division of the Indian peninsula by the Indus. And thus by a chain of circumstances subsequent to its decline, a name given by an imperial race to the boundary river of its empire became the sign through which a local river bequeathed its name to two hemispheres.

The sovereignty of the 'King River' is indeed anomalous. Without the sanctity of the Ganges, the Tapti or the Nerbudda, though it possess its Khwajah Khizr and its Daryâpanthis; royal but not holy. To the West a stream of ill-known parts long after the Ganges had become a familiar association; withal the partner of a valley that, save as a portal to India's immigrants and conquerors, has played an obscure rôle, the Indus has yet by the accidents of fortune and position acquired an imperial sway. And it is not the least strange aspect of this sovereignty that the river, its source, its delta, and even its

[1] The last division on the old lines was made by the treaty of 1739 between the Emperor of Delhi, Muhammad Shah, and Nadir Shah.

course, should have remained the subject of wildest error for centuries after its name had been given to a greater whole; that the ages that found Indies in the West or sought them by the North-West Passage should still bring the delta of the Indus to the Gulf of Cambay, and place one of its most ancient ports in Mekran.

IV

THE RAN OF CUTCH

THE RAN OF CUTCH. I

Of all the manifold features of the earth that have enchained man with terror, the desert promises to be the last to surrender to realism its atmosphere of romance. The oceans have given up the secrets of their vastness; the mountains have unveiled their innermost mystery; and the ice-poles can no longer serve as a retreat for lawless dreaming. Alone the desert remains a bridge between antiquity, with its fear of the grander forms of Nature, and our modern age with its romance that has superseded fear. Its plagues still engender a comprehended fear; its monochrome still suggests a latent force that evades controlling; and there lingers round its expanse something of the old doubt that made its sounds and sights not seldom of another world. The mirage is its sign—creation of relentless facts, product of great heat and aridity, yet withal seductive in the homage it pays to a universal willingness to welcome a semblance of the unreal.

The western coast of India has shared in many a romantic fancy, but the Ran of Cutch remains, in legend and in fact, the most attractive feature of the coast. To most it has few associations that are not the very breath of story. It is a desert of sterile decay, swept from time to time by monsoon and wave. Alexander marched along its shores; the Sultan Mahmud of Ghazni, and after him another, wandered with an army lost in its sun-drenched wastes, where no bird ever flapped its wings, no tree was to be seen, not a blade of grass or even a noxious weed.

Errors as to its history have been many. Burnes thought that its formation from an inland sea was due to the receding of the sea; McMurdo that it was an elevated sea-bottom; whilst the belief that it is still swept at times by a sea driven before the monsoon still abides. The appeal of the story of Sultan Mahmud of Ghazni in the eleventh century being warned, in his crossing the Ran to the Fort of Randama on one of its north-eastern islands, that he might be carried away by the tide, is so insidious as to suggest that its memory is still largely responsible for the popular belief that the Ran is a seasonal victim of the monsoon.

Our knowledge of the formation of the Ran has advanced *pari passu* with that of the rivers of Sind, and this has been attained so slowly that it is only some three decades since first the Ran was accepted as the delta of the Hakra, the great river that ran along the eastern boundary of Sind, already divorced of some of its tributaries in the tenth century, losing still more in the fourteenth century, and its last associate in the eighteenth. Thus the Hakra slowly deposed as the great fructifier of Sind, the Indus flowing through the centre of the valley has assumed its rôle. It is in the consequences of this great change that the history of the Ran is contained, and it is in the period during which this change was being effected that we can trace most clearly the stages in the drying up[1] of the inland sea which preceded the desert of to-day.

The *Periplus of the Erythræan Sea* described the sea in the two bays of the Ran, or Eirinos, as shallow with continual eddies and shoals. For centuries later there is evidence that the Ran remained navigable; later than the eighth century towns were founded near Nagar, in the most inland corner of the Greater Ran, the remains of which indicate prosperous ports, and of which one, Balmir, gives proof that the Luni, now blocked and silted at its mouth, was once navigable. Burnes gathered traditions that made ports of Vingar, Baliar and other towns, and of Pactram, an island looking inward upon the Ran, a shelter for storm-tossed vessels; whilst McMurdo found stone anchors far from the Ran and a native craft of the design moulded by the Arabs two thousand years ago.

When Sultan Firoz Shah crossed the Ran (A.D. 1362) it was apparently in part at least dry and firm, for his army wandered therein for days, and we hear of no such story as we are told of Sultan Mahmud and the tidal sea.

The change preserved in the very name of Ran was accompanied by a change in the delta of the Sind river; the shifting of the main river of the valley from its eastern limits

[1] According to Lassen the drying up of the inland sea is referred to in the *Mahabharata*, the disaster being placed to the credit of the god Varuna. Major-General Haigh records an old tradition that it was due to the curse of a holy man.

to its medial regions hastened the formation of the Indus delta, and yet more gave it a new direction. Successively abandoning the line that recorded the coast at the time of the Greeks, and advancing in stages beyond the limits that marked the delta in the eighth and sixteenth centuries, the delta of the Indus gradually came down almost to the frontier of Cutch, and well-nigh closed any ingress to the Ran on the north.

With this great transformation in the deltaic region of Sind the history of the Ran[1] must henceforward have a course far different from its past. The Ran is now a dried-up sea, the creation of alluvial deposits by rivers that have played their part once and for all. The Luni is now silted up, its mouth bordered by sand hills and a great salt lake; the Hakra has ceased to be a perennial stream, and the mouth of the Indus, a hundred miles further west, is well beyond the Ran. Its history, therefore, as the gradual silting up of an inland sea by the alluvium of rivers is now ended; a new history has opened in the process begun, whereby æolian deposits, carried by the wind from the desert of Thar and Parkar, will inevitably obliterate the processes of the past.

[1] *Journal of the Royal Geographical Society*, May, 1907, 'Cutch and the Ran,' by R. Sivewright, F.R.G.S.

THE RAN OF CUTCH. II

Shorn of all the fantastic and legendary signs that mark the post-Renaissance maps; shorn of its two great rivers, the Indus and Ganges, flowing due south from north; its islands, Kathiawar and Ceylon, reduced from their absurd and mythical proportion; its seas no longer one great circumambient or inland water; the map of India to-day would hardly seem a measure of error. And yet in one detail it perpetuates an error of centuries, and pays unwilling testimony to the obscurity that has surrounded a portion of India's coast for two thousand years. For the Ran of Cutch, neglected and unstudied, still figures in many a map, otherwise meticulously exact, as an arm of the sea associated in a partnership it lost long since.

Its contour, too, suggests a perverted value as a barrier to movement, that the Ran, in fine, has been as great a force as it is now an axiom to believe the desert of Rajputana and the Indus to have been, in segregating the valley of the Indus. For the Ran has been no such dividing factor. The separateness of the valley that finds a memory in the title 'India' transferred from the part to the whole, that has left a recollection of an age-long division of Sind and Hind in the expression 'Indies', and to the nomenclature of the nineteenth century transmitted an inheritance of Persian and Arab that drew from a consciousness of the barrier Indus—this proclaims the influence of the desert and the river. But though it now appears a bulwark even more imposing and minatory than the desert, though since the fourteenth century tradition has made of it an abode of desolation approaching death, the semblance of the Ran belies its real significance. From the dim days of the Dravidian to the eleventh and twelfth century migrations from Sind that peopled Cutch and Kathiawar; from the legends that brought Alexander along its coast to the plains of Gujarat, to the bardic annals that demonstrate a constant strife between the rulers of Sind and Gujarat until the latter passed under the empire of Delhi, the Ran has been no obstacle to migration or to conquest, and with the great desert can have no issue.

Yet if the seclusion of the Indus valley in history be due to the desert and not even in measurable part to the Ran, the latter has been the greatest of factors in concealing its real features from Western knowledge, and there is no part of India in respect to which Europe has indulged in such a riot of geographical errors as the short coast-line from Karachi to Cambay. Traditions, with little relation even in origin to reality, in survival defiant of repeated correction and heedless of anachronism, over a period of some two thousand years have cast an atmosphere of shade over a coast that still remains in popular knowledge ill-defined and vague. To the Ran the Indus owes the traditions that have, on the one hand, divorced it from the river of its ancient port, Debal, and on the other brought its mouth into the Gulf of Cambay ; from the Ran again Kathiawar has taken the stories that have made of it an island, and Cutch the confusion that has confounded it with Kathiawar or left it dwarfed to a few islets on the eastern coast of a deepened bight. To one and the same factor, in short, is due the long record that brings the Indus in a course due south from north, that locates its ancient port, Debal, in the barren surroundings of Mekran, and makes play for centuries with the latitude and longitude of the principal sites of Sind.

Of this riot of imagining and the persistence with which traditions that had become purely literary survived the correction by experience, the seventeenth and eighteenth centuries are rich in examples. Forecast of the confusion of these centuries is the report of Sir Edward Michelborne, borne in 1607 to the East India Company, on the advantages of the trade of the Indus, in which he describes Cutch (Jeketta) as within the mouth of the Indus.

A few years later the Company issued its instructions to Fremlen and to Sir Henry Middleton, and still a little later, with the landing of the 'Expedition' at Diul (1613), began the practical acquaintance of the West with the intricacies of the Indus delta. To the Company's servants in Sind the ports of the Indus henceforth became well known, as were the features of the Gulf of Cambay to those at Surat, in the Presidency of which the factors of Sind remained ; Bornford and Wylde sailed the whole course of the Indus from Lahore to the sea, to test its convenience for traffic, and even more the land route, that led through Jasalmir, was examined for its possible alternative advantages. From Gujarat Sir Thomas Roe (1615) and Pietro Della Valle reported the absence of the Indus from that province, and as a confusion due to swollen inundation or the course of the Mahi ridiculed the current errors of Mercator and others, who brought the mighty Indus into the Gulf of Cambay. Sir Thomas Roe further emphasised that the river that passed Tatha and Lahribandar was really the Indus, and not a separate river. And yet the repetition of history was the same. . Nicolo de Conti's more accurate description, in the fifteenth century, of the Gulf of Cutch and Cambay had not prevented Varthema from bringing the Indus near to Cambaia, nor Maffei from speaking of the '*bicornis Indus*' entering the sea in the kingdom of Cambay. The sixteenth century closes the record of Western knowledge with a chapter of absurdest errors. Barbosa had put the kingdom of Debal in Persia and made the Indus a tributary of the Euphrates, and the second Borgian map had brought the Indus direct south into the Gulf of Cambay in a course parallel to the Ganges; the identity of Cutch and Kathiawar had been confused, and of the two an island made and placed in the delta of the Indus. But almost each and every of these traditions was carried on by the seventeenth century, despite all its experience, into the next century, and wellnigh into the nineteenth.

The tradition that the Indus entered the Gulf of Cambay,[1] a consequent no doubt of a confusion of the waters that subsequently became the Ran, reminiscent of a time when the great river of Sind had a more easterly course than now, and a continuation of its waters across the Ran with an outlet by the Nal between Kathiawar and Gujarat, was not an imagining too vain, survived until the last. In origin an echo, perhaps, of the

[1] A familiar feature of Sind legend is the babe put in a basket or box after the manner of Moses, and abandoned to the river. The wanderings of these derelict babies take them to many strange places, which give the Indus among other routes one through Rajputana to Kathiawar. (*Tales of Old Sind*, Kincaid.)

The *Brahmaanada Purana* says the Indus flowed through the country of the Abhiras. The *Mahabharata* says the Abhiras lived near the coast and on the bank of the Sarasvati. The Aberia of the Greeks is identified with the south-eastern portion of Gujarat and the river Sarasvati with a river near Somnath.

classic idea that made so many rivers flow direct south from north, an echo more confused again of Ptolemy's map which makes a continuous coast from Mekran to Cambay, and places Saurashtra in the delta of the Indus; corrected in the fifteenth century, again proved false in the sixteenth, it is still accepted by Fryer (1676), who speaks of the Indus falling into the bottom of the Gulf of Cambay; and by Hamilton, who later regards Gujarat as the country next to Sind made insular by an arm of the Indus.

And the other tradition so intimately connected with this, that the river of Debal was a separate river, the Rio de Diul of Van Linschoten, had a similar course. Exposed by the experience of the East India Company, exposed by Sir Thomas Roe, the river of Debal remains a river apart until interest in its position has ceased. In the maps that illustrate the earlier editions of Mandelslo, Harris, or again Pietro Della Valle and Bernier, it is a river in Mekran sometimes bearing the name Ilmand or Ibnent. And, emphatic of the way in which traditions were unexamined and passed on, is Hamilton's *New Account*, for Hamilton knew the delta between Tatha and Lahribandar, yet places an imaginary mouth of the Indus in the Gulf of Cambay and repeats the location of Debal in Mekran. Of all the absurdities that the Ran of Cutch has occasioned, there is none equal to that which took out of the limits of Sind a port famous for its wealth until at least the thirteenth century and placed it in Mekran.

And there lingered yet other errors that suggest an affinity with the past. Ptolemy's coast was a deltaic coast from Sind to Cambay, running from west to east; the coast of the Arab maps of the tenth century is the straightest of lines from Mekran to Cambay, whilst the Arab historian-geographers describe a coastal stretch of salty waste from Debal to Cambay along which was a well-recognised highway of travel, but make no reference to Cutch till the eleventh century. And the later representation of Cutch as a few islets within a deepened bight that brings the mouths of the Indus up to the northern edge of Kathiawar is one that differs little from the written account of Al Idrisi.

A Golfe de Indus, Golfe D' India, is in the seventeenth

century maps the substitute for the Ran of Cutch; in many a map this is bare of islands save those that, in the very proximity of Tatha, carry the alluvial coast of Sind further south; in others the present islands of Cutch are missing on the western side of the Ran and in their place a row of islets fringe the eastern coast. And that eastern coast, somewhat after the manner of Ptolemy's map, includes Soreth and even Cutch, whilst south of the River Paddar a Kathiawar, including part of the modern Cutch, struggles between a desire to be an island and remain a peninsula. In yet further details this Ran is prolific of errors; the rivers that flow into the Ran between Cambay and the Indus produce endless confusion, and when the Indus is not confused with the Mahi or does not retain its own separate course, it is amalgamated with the Paddar and flows from north-east along the northern boundary of Kathiawar.

Futile and absurd, however, as most of these extravagances doubtless are, it is their survival up to the nineteenth century that is their strangest feature. Rennell, in 1793, remarks in his Memoir that the Gulf of Cutch has been found less than and Kathiawar much larger than erstwhile supposed. Exact and true, it is yet a strange comment upon two centuries of geographical knowledge. Up to the very end the maps that accompany editions of Sir Thomas Herbert and Mandelslo show Cutch and Kathiawar as a single island of queerest shape; with naïve impartiality a single edition of Mandelslo shows, in 1720, the Indus flowing due south into the Gulf of Cambay and again into the sea north of the peninsula of Kathiawar. And amid all these cartographical misrepresentations of the chief features of the Ran there run the absurdest locations of the ports and towns of the Indus valley which a distorted course of the river required; an utter confusion of names duplicated at pleasure, a conjectural location, and even an amalgamation of, others adds bewilderment to confusion, and there is no theory of identity of the respective ports of the delta that cannot find cartographical evidence in its support.

In the history of error there is assuredly nothing more striking than the tardiness with which Europe gained even an approximately accurate idea of the main features of India. The Renaissance, that added so largely to the knowledge of the world, that dissipated so many misconceptions of the cosmos and made for ever impossible a revival of the more obvious crudities of mediæval maps, worked its reformation with strange slowness in the correction of traditions as to the geography of western India.

Still in the seventeenth century Sir Thomas Herbert, Fryer and Mandelslo can think of the Western and Eastern Ghats as a single ridge of mountains running, as do the Appennines in Italy, from north to south of the peninsula; Sir Thomas Herbert can still talk of the Caucasus on the bound of India, and still describe the delta of the Indus through the medium of names dead since the time of Alexander. And even beyond this century run with unabated vigour the traditions that make the Indus flow into the Gulf of Cambay, that make of Kathiawar an island and the whole coast from Mekran to Cambay the delta of the Indus. And the cause of the major part of these errors, the Ran, retains in record the same features as the Arab accounts of the tenth century would give, and nearly those that Ptolemy would have rendered.

Strangest of all is the failure of Sir Thomas Roe and Pietro Della Valle to correct the maps of the delta; equally strange the rebuke given by Mandelslo to authors who wrongly placed the Indus twenty-four degrees from true, confounding it with the river of Debal; the robbing from Sind of its ancient port and the facile repetition of traditions, long since falsified, by Hamilton when writing beyond the limit of his own experience.

V

DEBAL

DEBAL

THERE is a semblance of stage-setting in the record of Sind history, for across its pages, as across a stage, flit creations that are with us awhile and then gone. Over their coming and their going we have no control; spectators at the mercy of the playwright, we can rarely follow the life-line of a single one from its birth to its close. And in nothing is shown a greater disrespect for continuity than in the meteoric flashes that reveal for a time new centres of history, and the sudden eclipses that end their days. The origins of the major part of the ancient sites of the valley are lost in impenetrable obscurity. None can tell how or when arose Alor, Sehwan, Debal, or even the thirteenth century Bakhar; and the inability to say when the names of Mansura, Debal, and Alor are mere echoes from the dead is no less bewildering than the abruptness with which a Bahmanabad or a Damrilah disappears. In repeating *in parvo* these main characteristics of a larger stage, Debal succeeds in offering us the tragedy of problems that baffle solution, and the comedy of errors in solving them.

In the long-drawn controversy as to the identity of Debal and its location there is no small element of humour. Great is the irony of assumptions that have justified a location both at Karachi and near Tatha; and the interpretation of record that has made Debal in succession an inland town, a port upon the sea, a town upon the Indus, and a distant neighbour thereto. Among the many locations[1] of old Debal as a

[1] Locations of Debal gather round Tatha or Karachi. Those that are impressed by the sterile surroundings of Debal, and seek a coastal port on the assumption of an unchanged delta, place it near Karachi. Bamburah (Hughes, Ranking); Karachi (Elliot); vicinity of Karachi (A. Burnes, Elphinstone). Others follow native tradition and find it in Tatha (Burton, Pottinger, Sir A. Burnes, Capt. McMurdo, De la Rochette, Rennell, W. Hamilton). The same sites have been given to Debal and Bahmanabad, though both places are mentioned in the *Chachnama* (e.g. Tod's 'Tatha'; Sir A. Burnes' 'Kalankot'; Wood's 'Tatha'). More independent locations are Maj.-Gen. Haigh's 'Kukar Bukera', 20 miles S.-W. of Tatha, apparently assumed proven by Mr. Dames; Raverty's near the shrine of Pir Patho, at the foot of the Makhli hills. Raverty identifies Sindi and Debal. Cunningham and Mr. Foster identify it with Lahribandar, Mr. Dames makes it a joint port with Sindi.

separate port there is none not based upon an initial error of assumption, or an erroneous reading of record, and almost all are vitiated by the assumption that the delta has always been much as it is to-day. Equally confusing are the respective identities of Tatha, Debal, Sindi, Lahribandar, and the solutions offered to reduce their number; the common but now discredited identification of Tatha and Debal; that of Debal and Sindi by Raverty; of Debal and Lahribandar by Cunningham and Mr. Foster; of Sindi and Lahribandar by Irvine and Yule; and again the recognition of all four by Mr. Dames. The very mass

The errors of assumption in these locations are many. Maj.-Gen. Haigh assumes that all the deltaic ports were originally inland, and so locates Debal by calculation of measurements given by the Arabs from other sites and, as he regards them, from the river's mouth inland. Yet Ibn Haukal puts Debal upon the sea, and Ibn Batuta Lahori upon the seashore.

Cunningham assumes that Debal was on the Indus—sequitur his identification with Lahribandar or ruins near by, yet the *Istakhari* puts it west of the mouth of the Mihran as does Ibn Haukal. Al Idrisi puts it six miles west of the mouth, and, earlier than all, Al Masudi puts it two days' journey west. From Hamilton's naming the Indus 'Divellae', or seven mouths, he makes the inconsequent deduction that the river of Lahribandar and that of Debal are one. Elliot places Debal near or at Karachi, on an assumption that the delta has ever been as it is. This compels him to seek a sterile hinterland near the sea, to suit the position of old Debal on the sea and the descriptions given of its surroundings by the Arab writers. Cf. Ibn Haukal.

Debal is a confined place (barren), but for the sake of trade people take up their dwelling there. They cultivate the land without irrigation.

Debal is a populous place but not fertile, and is inhabited merely because it is a harbour for the vessels of Sind and other parts (Al Idrisi).

When Rai Dahir heard of its fall (A.D. 711) he made light of it, saying it was a place inhabited by low people and traders.

Mr. M. L. Dames (*vide* Duarte Barbosa) makes a joint port out of Deval and Sindi, and puts Dewal where Maj.-Gen. Haigh places it. Lahribandar he puts in the extreme east of the delta. Reasons for any one of these locations which result in accepting as separate towns each and every of the places mentioned in record are not given. As I have shown in the text, Lahribandar could never have been in the alluvial east of the delta.

The maps of the seventeenth and eighteenth centuries have a location of Debal which is comparatively unbalanced by written record. Barbosa puts Diul result in the sovereignty of Persia; Hamilton puts Debal in Mekran; the former incidentally makes the Indus come from the Euphrates and the latter makes it enter the Gulf of Cambay. In maps it is frequently located in Mekran. The location is inseparable from the erroneous idea that the river of Debal was a different river from the Indus—Sir Thomas Roe corrected the error; Garcia da Orta, almost a century earlier, wrote that the Indo is called by the natives Diul, yet Mandelslo refused an identification of Van Linschoten's Aio de Diul with the Indus, and Debal continued to be put in Mekran with a river of its own up to the nineteenth century. A location based upon a belief that the Indus entered the sea in the Gulf of Cambay, and upon recollection that the hinterland of old Debal was desert and that this was not to be found in the alluvial precincts of the later parts, is an extravagance of tradition that does not call for detailed criticism.

of error and conflict alone would justify an attempt to reach simplicity.

By way of introduction to a subject with many difficulties, let us turn to a century, the seventeenth, in which we have happily a fund of contemporary evidence as to the identity of the ports of the Indus delta, from travellers and historians who write of personal experience. The author of the *Tarikh-i-Tahiri* went to Tatha in A.D. 1606 for his education, and at Tatha lived part of his later life. In 1635 the 'Discovery' landed Fremlen and Forder at 'Laurebandar'; in 1654 Tavernier arrived at Sindi at the mouth of the river; one year later Manucci landed at the port of Sindi and thence reached the towns of Sindi and Tatha; in 1699 Hamilton travelled with peril, for his caravan was attacked, from Lahribandar to Tatha. In addition, this century furnishes the reports of the East India Company's factors at Tatha.

Now all these authorities agree in describing one port only other than Tatha, with factories of two or three nationalities. The distance of Lahribandar from the sea, and again from Tatha, given by the *Tarikh-i-Tahiri*, by Fremlen and Hamilton, are too similar to those given by Manucci to Sindi to make doubtful an identification[1] of Sindi with Lahribandar. A further simplification of the number of ports is a result of the various reports

[1] Sindi as Lahribandar :—

Tarikh-i-Tahiri.	Lahribandar,	one day from sea, two days from Tatha.
Fremlen.	"	14 miles up river.
Hamilton.	"	six leagues from sea (40 miles).
Manucci.	Sindi	12 hours up river (36 miles).

Sindi is put by Terry (1618) at the mouth of the main current of the river, i.e. at the mouth of the same branch as Lahribandar. Forder, describing a landing at Bandarlarrye, says they sighted high, rugged land to the west of Cindy (1635). There was possibly a small anchorage called Sindi, or something like it, at the very mouth of the river; Manucci writes of Dara Shukoh crossing the river from the port to the town of Sindi; John Spiller (1646) writes from Sindy Road, which is distinct from Lahribandar (Bandar). Others locate a small village at the actual mouth of the river, e.g. *Tarikh-i-Tahiri*, Sommiani; Fremlen, a poor fisher town; Hamilton puts a Sindi Tower at the mouth. Fremlen has also a 'Sinda Road' distinct from Lahribandar. No Oriental historian to my knowledge uses the title Sindi as the name of a port; by Europeans it is frequently used to indicate Tatha and Lahribandar alike (*vide The English Factories in India*, W. Foster, 1618-94) and occasionally an anchorage, but not a real port at the mouth of the river.

Paynton calls his Diul (the 'Lowrebandar' of Kerridge and Withington) also Diulsinde.

Thevenot has also Diul-Sind. Sidi Ali Kapudan identifies Lahori with Diul Sind.

made of the landing[1] of Sir Robert Shirley and others in Sind in A.D. 1613; for Paynton, the master of the ship that carried them, names the port Diul; Kerridge, reporting a little later the landing, calls the port Laurebendar, as does also Withington, who on hearing of the same proceeded overland from Surat in an ill-fated attempt to help the new arrivals. The evidence, in fact, that Lahribandar[2] was the only deltaic port at this time other than Tatha is overwhelming. Its pre-eminence is shown by Mir Ma'asumi's inscription of its name, as one of the dependent cities of the Emperor Akbar, in a recess cut in a hill of Kandahar, and at least the importance of its position by the reservation to the Emperor of Hindusthan of its castle town in the treaty of 1739 with Nadir Shah.

Still more than this the record of this century permits of a location of Lahribandar with every appearance of probable accuracy. The landing from the 'Discovery' of Fremlen and Forder gives us a description of the river's mouth near Lahribandar; we are told that before reaching anchorage they sighted high cliffs that in the light appeared to the west as chalk cliffs, and passed an island entered in the charts as 'Camel', the coast itself at the river's mouth low lying without

[1] 'In November, 1613, the Expedition arrived at Laurebander, the port of Sinda, and there disembarked Sir Robert Shirley and his company' (Letters received by the E. I. Co., vol. II, No. 165—Thomas Kerridge to the E. I. Co., 20th September, 1614).

'Boats were sent from Diul for conveying to the ambassadors goods and people . . . Tata, a great citie one dayes journey from Diul, both cities standing in the Great Mogolls Dominions, the ship was riding about four or five miles from the river's mouth from whence they had fifteen miles to the city or town of Diul . . . they went through the city to the castle.' The party proceeding from Diul to Tatha were brought back and 'carried away prisoners to Diulsinde.'

[2] *Vide* information given by Sir Edward Michelborne in interview with Co., as entered in the court minutes of January 26th, 1607-8: 'Lawrie in the Bay of the River Syndu,' Sir Thomas Herbert. 'Tatha . . . upon the ocean she has Laurebandar.' John Jourdain left England on E. I. Co. Fourth Voyage. The Commanders had instructions, if Surat was unsafe, to have recourse to Lahribandar at the mouth of the Indus.

Thevenot distinguishes the most southern town Diul, Diul-Sind ('heretobefore called Dobil') from 'Lourebandar', which is three days' journey from Tatha upon the sea. Thevenot, however, never visited Sind; Tavernier did at the same time that Thevenot was in India (1665-66); he arrived at Sindi and speaks only of Sindi and Tatha. It is always necessary, in interpreting accounts of the deltaic ports, to separate the records of personal experience from those of hearsay; Hamilton, an authority on the part he knew between Lahribandar and Tatha, is none when he speaks of Debal in Mekran, or a second branch of the Indus debouching into the Gulf of Cambay.

a distinguishing feature save a single tree. Over sixty years later Hamilton in very similar manner describes the difficulty of finding the mouth of a river, which had only a whitened tower over a tomb as a guiding mark; and adds the further information that the port had a fort and mounted guns, to protect its trade from the attacks of Baluchi and Mekrani robbers to the west. There are here, accordingly, several fairly precise indications as to the location of Lahribandar; it was within sight of cliffs or hills, itself on a formless shore at the mouth of a river that was presumably the river of Debal, as the Camel island can hardly be other than the 'Camello' island that appears in so many maps, and in the early English translation of Van Linschoten, at the mouth of the river of Debal. It is quite impossible to satisfy these conditions of location by any situation in the alluvial stretches of the eastern delta; and only possible somewhere along the edge of the rocky desert, that in the Karachi district adjoins on the north the deltaic accretions of lower levels.

In yet one more respect the seventeenth century enables us to reach assurance where so much is doubt. In the extensive use of the name 'Sindi'[1] is a refutation of much error. In 1631 Philip Lukaszoon speaks of the Brouwershaven being sent to 'Tata, named Sindi in the charts'; Tavernier speaks of Sindi as the capital of the province of Tatha, i.e. as Tatha itself. Sindi is used by Manucci and Bernier to indicate the town of Lahribandar, and by Manucci a separate anchorage at the mouth of the river. And similar in detail is the use of the name 'Sinda.' Methwold, in a letter of 1636, writes of Tatha *alias* Sinda; Kerridge speaks of 'Laurebandar' as the port of Sinda, i.e. of Tatha; Fremlen speaks of Tatha as 'Scinda'; in 1629 the Committee receives a report that 'Synda' (Tatha)

[1] Mir Ma'asumi speaks of a hill at Kandahar with a recess cut by order of the Emperor Babar. 'When I visited the spot it came into my head that I would inscribe his (Humayun's) name there, as well as that of his august son, with their thousands of tributary cities and kingdoms like Kandahar and Kabul. I therefore sent for some stone-cutters and engravers from Bakhar, and had the names of these kings engraved, with those of their dependent cities and provinces from Bengal to Bandar Lahori, from Kabul and Ghazni to the Dekhan, without any omission. It took nearly four years to complete this work.'

'The castle and town of Lahribandar, with all the countries to the east of the river Attok, the water of Sind and Nala Sankra shall, as formerly, belong to the Empire of Hindustan' (Treaty of Nadir Shah, 1739).

is soliciting the Surat President to found a factory there. The same name is also used, though not quite so frequently, for Lahribandar, whilst when the port of Synda or a ship of Synda is mentioned in the letters and reports of the Company's presidents, factors and captains it is not always possible to say whether Tatha or Lahribandar is meant.

Now the *Tarikh-i-Ma'asumi* is dubbed ignorant by Elliot because its author speaks of Lahribandar and Tatha as both called Debal, but this is at the beginning of the century, when there is ample proof that in European use Sindi was similarly employed as a name for these two. This duplication of Sindi also makes seem less strange the statement of the *Tuhfat-ul-Kiram* that Bandar-Lahori was of old called Bandar-Debal, for with the Persian izafat in its proper place, becoming 'Bandar-i-Debal', Bandar Debal may mean either the port Lahribandar, i.e. port Diul or Sindi, or again the port belonging to the town of Tatha, called equally Debal or Sindi (Sinda).

Yet more than this, this indiscriminating use of the names Sindi and Sinda weakens the conclusion of Mr. Foster that Debal and Lahribandar were one. In support of this conclusion, he remarks that in the early English accounts reference is made only to the one (Diul) or the other (Lahribandar), never to both; that it seems incredible that there could have been at the same time two cities at the mouth of the Indus, each serving as a port of Tatha, and each containing a Portuguese factory, and that the port which Paynton calls 'Diul', Withington and Kerridge call 'Lowribandar'. Now Diul is but one half of Diul-Sindi, and if the use of Diul as a name for Lahribandar is support for an identification of these two places, the common use of Sindi (Sinda), the other half of Diul-Sindi, equally justifies an assumption that Debal and Tatha were one.

It is easier now to turn to the detailed record of Debal itself. Of the survival of the name Debal up to recent times there is no doubt. The instructions of the East India Company's Committee to Femell, and again to Sir Henry Middleton in 1610, suggest the founding of a factory at 'Dabul'; Paynton, as related above, calls Diul the port at which Sir Robert Shirley landed in 1613; Crow, the British Agent at Tatha in 1799, writes of Tatha as 'Debal Sindi' and even of two ruined sites in the delta of the same name Major Raverty,[1] the staunchest advocate of the triple identity of Tatha,[2] Debal, and Lahribandar quotes the landing of the author of the *Jahanara* at Debal in 1567, and the statement of the *Khalasat-ut-Tawarikh* that Debal was the chief

[1] Major Raverty's notes on Debal, Tatha and Lahribandar, despite their learning, are unconvincing. He places the last on the Bhagar branch of the Indus, and accepts its position thereon in the seventeenth century as some 20 miles from the mouth; he emphasises that the Lahari of Ibn Batuta was at a junction of the river with the sea eastward of Debal; he also in places accepts from Al Beruni a distance of twelve farsakhs between Debal and Loharani. Inconsistent with this, he definitely locates Debal near Pir Patho, i.e. east of any possible port at the mouth of the Bhagar, and having in one place read the twelve farsakhs of Al Beruni as measured from Debal to Loharani, he elsewhere reads it as between Debal and the most eastern mouth (Kohrai) of the Indus, rejecting altogether apparently the reading of 'Loharani'.

His precise measurement of Debal from Tatha is a misreading of Paynton's account, for the latter does not say that Diul was fifteen miles from Tatha, but that distance from the river's mouth. His examples of the survival of Debal as more than a name are unfortunate. Sir Thomas Herbert did not land at Diul but at Swalley Road; Paynton's Diul is most certainly Lahribandar, as is also Terry's 'Sindee'. Thevenot cannot be balanced against the authority of those who visited Sind, nor the *Khalasat-ut-Tawarikh* against that of the resident historians of Sind.

[2] *Tatha and Debal.* Major Raverty, who believes Debal existed after the foundation of Tatha, can give authentic references to the former up to A.D. 1224, when Sultan Jalaluddin invaded lower Sind. It is then significant that he has no instance of Debal to offer after this date until A.D. 1567; i.e. on his assumption that Debal survived up to the end of the seventeeth century there is a silence of some 350 years in the record of Debal.

As regards Tatha, he assumes from Ibn Batuta's silence as to the existence of Tatha when he was at Lahribandar, 1333-34, that Tatha did not then exist; like Maj.-Gen. Haigh, he finds the first reference to Tatha in Barni's account of the pursuit to Tatha and the banks of the Indus of the rebel Taghi by the Sultan Muhammad Shah in 1351. Raverty further says that Tatha was founded by the son of Jam Unar, who bore the title of *Bani-i-Tatha*, or 'Founder of Tatha', and succeeded Jam Junan in A.D. 1349-50.

Ibn Batuta apparently only describes the places he visited, as he kept to the river; perhaps Tatha was a place to avoid in 1333, maybe it was not on the river. The existence of a title so distinctive as 'Founder of Tatha' would make very difficult of explanation the subsequent obscurity as to the origin of Tatha, and the crediting of its foundation by the *Tarikh-i-Tahiri*, the author of which was a Sammah and a resident of Tatha, to Jam Nindo at the end of the fifteenth century. Further than this the *Tarikh-i-Firoz Shahi* of Shamsi Siraj Afif, the author of which knew the court of the Emperor Firoz Shah if not the sites of his campaign in the Indus delta, says that the brother of Jam Unarand Babiniya (the latter the name that by reason of its many variant readings in MSS., Raverty makes into 'Bani' or 'Founder') were taken as hostages to Delhi, where they had a Tatha palace at their disposal; that the former was sent back to Tatha to quell a rebellion, but that the latter never saw Tatha again, as when later he, too, was sent back with the present of an umbrella, he died on the way: the 'Bani' or 'Founder' thus fades away into a personal name of a chief.

To Tatha I would give a much earlier date than 1350; even than 1333, the date of Ibn Batuta's visit to Sind. To leave contemporary history for the moment, there is quite a considerable amount of historical record of various value

port of Sind in the days of Aurangzeb. The survival of the name, however, does not prove the survival of the city, and of even plausible proof that the city continued after 1350 there would seem to be none. In the seventeenth century there is certainly no reference to a Debal by those who knew themselves the ports of the delta, save by Hamilton, and he, placing Debal in Mekran, beyond the limits of his personal experience, demonstrates that he, too, knew of no Debal in the delta.

When exactly the old Debal ceased to be is not easy to say. In 1205 Nasiruddin Kabajah possessed himself of Sind as far as the coast, but Debal, under a Sumrah chief, remained in semi-independence. In 1224 the same Sumrah chief left Debal in flight before the Sultan Jalaluddin, and this is, Maj.-Gen. Haigh considers, one of the latest, if not the latest, notice of Debal. It is thus as a Sumrah possession that it fades from record, and personally I have little doubt that the end of Debal is wrapped in obscurity, because it is one incident in that conflict of Sumrah

that associates Tatha with the campaigns of emperors earlier than Sultan Muhammad Shah Taghlak. Badaoni says that the eldest son of the Emperor Ghiyassuddin (1266-1286) conquered Tatha and Damrilah; traditions that connect Tatha with Sultan Ala-ud-din are more numerous; the *Tuhfat-ul-Kiram* brings in this Sultan to wipe out the Sumrahs; the *Tarikh-i-Ma'asumi* also brings him to Tatha, whilst to-day there remain as an object of worship at Tatha the reputed tombs of seven royal Sumrah dames, who committed suicide rather than fall into his hands. But what is greater than all, there is the testimony of the *Tarikh-i-Firoz Shahi* of Shamsi Siraj. Describing the defeat of the Jams of Tatha in 1362 by Sultan Firoz Shah, he writes thus: 'Tatha had been a source of trouble to the sovereigns of Delhi ever since the days of Sultan Muizzuddin. . . . The splendid army of Sultan Ala-ud-din had marched towards Tatha, but the difficulty of the enterprise had rendered the attempt abortive. . . . Sultan Muhammad Shah Taghlak lost his life in the same country.'

Here then is evidence that in the reign of Firoz Shah Tatha traditionally had a history that took it back to the time of Sultan Ala-ud-din (1296-1315), if not into the days of Debal (A.D. 1182); and this evidence, with that of Barni, is the earliest reference to Tatha.

The *Gazetteer of Sind* relates that even in 1398 Tatha was not built, though historians used the name; apparently the evidence of the *Tuhfat-ul-Kiram*, completed 1767 or later, and for the most part a collection of legends, is preferred to that of Barni, who accompanied Sultan Muhammad Shah to Tatha in 1350.

The *Tarikh-i-Firoz Shahi* of Barni says Taghi went to Tatha and Damrilah; that the Sultan Muhammad Shah followed, with intention of humbling the Sumrahs, who had given him protection.

The *Tarikh-i-Ma'asumi* says Taghi conspired with the Sumrahs, and that Sultan Firoz Shah fought two battles with them before Taghi fled, and he himself was able to retire to Delhi.

The story that Tatha was founded by Jam Nandu Babiniya is repeated by Dr. Jivaji Jamshedji Modi, in the *Journal of the Bombay Branch of the Asiatic Society*, vol. xxiv, on the authority of the *Tarikh-i-Tahiri*.

and Sammah which is presented to us in melodramatic manner and with a plenitude of fictions.

Whatever the year in which Debal ceased as a city known to itself, it is significant that it has been left for the nineteenth century to quarrel over its remains. From the middle of the fourteenth century onwards native record has no doubts; no ruins in the delta are pointed out as those of the great Debal, more famous as it had been perhaps as a place of pilgrimage even than as an emporium of wealth, but Tatha is unanimously hailed as heir to the glory of Debal. As one of the cities of the accursed Sumrahs, it is difficult, too, to think that, had its days been ended by earthquake, sack, or even natural decay, the Sammah historian would have failed to point his inevitable moral, or sing his pæan of victory. The very sites of the Sumrah cities, we are told by the example of Muhammad Tur, were held accursed; the cultivation of the Sumrahs was allowed to go to waste, and the waste of their time became in turn fertility itself under the Sammahs. There seems therefore no reason why the Sammah should have spared the memory of Debal had it really not survived.

Surviving after the foundation of Tatha, Debal must of necessity have been Tatha or Lahribandar, and, as the use of 'Diul' and 'Sindi' ('Sinda') in duplicate for both Tatha and Lahribandar would support either the one identification or the other, it is on more general grounds that the question must be decided.

In the position I have given to Lahribandar,[1] a position accepted by the advocates of its identity with Debal, to assume

[1] *Lahribandar:—*

Ibn Batuta visited Lahari in 1334; he puts it at the mouth of the Sind river upon the sea-shore. Beyond saying it has a large harbour he gives of it no detailed description. Al Beruni (Rashiduddin) in the *Indika* has a 'Lahārani' for which he gives a synonym 'Lohaniyah'; the Arabic text of the *Indika* suggests that Debal is inland and on the main highway from Mekran to Cambay, and a convenient site from which to detail the distances of coastal and other places, *inter alia* Loharani.

I do not know of any subsequent mention of Lahribandar for two centuries. The *Tarikh-i-Ma'asumi* says the Khan-i-Khanan went to Lahribandar to see the sea; the *Tarikh-i-Tahiri* that the Portuguese, who sacked Tatha in A.D. 1565, landed at Lahribandar. Fremlen (1635) writes of it as a well-inhabited town, but its houses as built of mud and sticks in a manner that made it a wonder they did not fall; Hamilton (1699) describes it as a village of a hundred houses of mud and crooked sticks, but with a large stone fort.

that Lahribandar was built as successor to Debal, which an expanding delta had left far inland, is to explain its situation naturally at the mouth of a river still communicating with the more ancient port, for the historic superseding of port by port in the delta is a slow process of succession; the new port is always built ere the old one has entirely decayed, and the inheritance of the past is surrendered gradually.

There remains the identification of Tatha and Debal, and in this regard the evidence of native history has been somewhat unfairly treated, for, in scorning the evidence of the *Tarikh-i-Ma'asumi* and the *Tuhfat-ul-Kiram*, the duplicate use of 'Sindi'

Between 1334, when it was on the sea, and the sixteenth century, it had shared the fate of all the deltaic ports drawn from an advancing delta. Though often loosely described by the Company's servants as at the mouth of the Indus, it was at the beginning of the seventeenth century already some 14 miles from the sea, and a small village on the coast had a guard and Mirbandar, which regulated the passing of vessels of the river. Communication by the river with that village, or higher up with Tatha, remained difficult; the *Tarikh-i-Tahiri* describes the communication with the sea as a small unfordable channel. Fremlen writes of the dangerous bar that was really only passable when the land winds, between October and mid-February, kept it smooth; Spiller (1646) reports the difficulty in getting goods in boats from Tatha to Lahribandar, as, until the tide is met half-way between, the water in places is not a foot deep and boats have to be drawn by mere strength on poles; Methwold alludes to it being more frequent for boats to come down from Tatha to Lahribandar than to go upstream.

The importance of separating the records of experience from those that perpetuate traditions of the past is very clearly demonstrated by the conflicting accounts of the anchorage and harbourage afforded by Lahribandar in the seventeenth century. The dangers of its approach are constantly emphasised in the reports of the Company's factors; ships that lie there again are 'subject to the worm'; Tavernier (February, 1654) was compelled by high seas to leave the anchorage and seek moorings six leagues away; the English ships (1635) could not find their way in without the aid of Portuguese frigates: against all this unmistakable proof of the difficulties and dangers of the anchorage of Lahribandar there are accounts that I think merely represent a literary survival of traditions when Lahribandar had, as it had had in centuries before, a fine harbour. The only other explanation of the conflicting accounts is to assume a great change in a few years. At the beginning of the century Sir Edward Michelborne (1607-8) informed the Company that 'Laurie' had a 'good harbor in saffetie'; Nicholas Withington writes that it has 'a fair road without the river's mouth, clear of worms'; and Thevenot (1666) says it has 'a better road for ships than any other place in the Indies.'

Yet the evidence as to the silting up of the river's mouth is considerable. Aurangzeb attempted to open a new port, which Spiller and Scrivener (1652) name Cuckerhallah. In the very same year that Thevenot landed at Surat, Tavernier landed in Sind; he describes the dangerous shallows formed by silt, and testifies to the decay in the trade of Tatha. In the latter respect Thevenot endorses his account of the diversion of the river traffic that erstwhile went from Lahore to Tatha; and of the partial decay of Lahore and Multan in consequence of the damage done to trade by the extra cost now entailed in taking goods *via* Agra by land from Lahore to Surat.

and 'Sinda' was forgotten, and that of the Persian izafat imperfectly understood. In crediting, moreover, Ferishta with the sin of misleading generations, the weight of evidence in his support has been overlooked, for the evidence that reads backwards into the times of old Debal—the name of Tatha evincing as it does a prevalent belief that the two were one—is not even confined to those that wrote on Sind, and without going into the respective value as historical material of this or that record, it is sufficient to appraise rightly the mass of testimony to a belief that Tatha was Debal.

Before Ferishta there is Abu Fazl, who makes Tatha synonymous with Debal, and puts Lahribandar in the sirkar of Tatha; there is Mir Ma'asumi, who recognises only Tatha and Lahribandar with the common appellation of 'Debal'. In the Bhatti annals Tod has given evidence, from the bardic history of Jasalmir, of the application of the name Tatha to a capital of the twelfth century. In the *Ras Mala*, again, Forbes has collected many a story that carries Tatha back even to the days of Bahmanabad. The *Munatakhabu-i-Tawarikh* is yet another example of this backward reading of history, for long before Tatha was founded it speaks of that city in the thirteenth century, where other authority would have written of Debal; and definitely alludes to the synonymity of the two.

One might, in fine, multiply much illustration of the belief that Tatha was Debal, but this evidence has been so generally discredited of late that any independent corroboration of it is welcome. Now Debal fades away from record coupled mysteriously with the name of Damrilah,[1] and as a stronghold of the Sumrahs, and it is therefore singular that Tatha in its

[1] Damrilah is one of the puzzles of Sind record. Like Bakhar, it does not appear till the thirteenth century. It then invariably appears coupled with Debal; so coupled it is mentioned by the *Tabakat-i-Nasiri*, the *Jahan Kusha* and the *Jami-ut-Tawarikh* of Rashiduddin; when Tatha first appears in Barni's account of the Emperor Muhammad Shah's pursuit of the rebel Taghi into Sind, it is equally strangely coupled with Tatha. I know of no instance of its mention alone by any writer of the thirteenth and fourteenth centuries, though the *Muntakhabu-i-Tawarikh* of Badaoni writes of the conquest of Damrilah by the eldest son of the Sultan Ghiyasuddin. Major Raverty in one passage indentifies it with the ruins found by Ibn Batuta near Lohari, an identification made impossible by the later mention of Damrilah in the account of Taghi's rebellion; elsewhere he places it near Shakhrpur in the Shahbandar sub-division, where local traditions certainly still point to the debris of the residences of Sumrah chiefs, among them of Chanisar, whose name history and legend alike associates with Debal.

early historic mention is likewise coupled with the same Damrilah, and first appears in connection with the Sumrahs. For the incident of the flight of the rebel Taghi from Gujarat to Tatha and Damrilah, as given by Barni, who accompanied the Emperor Muhammad Taghlak in his fatal advance to the Indus, provides this continuity of detail, which can hardly be accidental.

If one adds to the evidence that Tatha, the Sammah capital of lower Sind, was at one time a Sumrah possession; that it is first mentioned with Damrilah, as was Debal, another Sumrah city; that of its founding there is no more authentic record than there is of the end of Debal, the discovery by Mr. Cousens on the Makhli hills of the remains of a fine Hindu temple, it is difficult to avoid a conclusion that here was really the Debal of old.

And now *en envoi* to touch finally upon the confused identities of Tatha, Lahribandar, Sindi and Debal. Mr. Dames, the latest writer (1918) to theorise upon their respective sites, makes of Lahribandar a port in the far east of the delta, and of Debal and Sindi a joint port on both sides of the western estuary of the river. In the record of the maps of the seventeenth and eighteenth centuries, indeed, support can be found for even this solution, which the whole weight of written experience would seem to render highly improbable.

It matters not for the moment whether Tatha was Debal or not; it suffices that the *Ain-i-Akbari*, the *Tarikh-i-Tahiri*, the *Tarikh-i-Ma'asumi* and the *Tuhfat-ul-Kiram*—of these three acquainted with Sind, and two residents of the delta—recognise no Debal apart. It matters not, equally, whether Sindi is Lahribandar or not, it is enough that no single traveller or factor who knew the Indus' mouths alludes to more than one port subsidiary to Tatha. Paynton may have his Diul; Tavernier and Manucci their Sindi; Hamilton and others their Lahribandar; the quotient remains the same—one capital and one port. And over these hangs a common name, for Sindi is but a name in duplicate; the silence of native record as to the existence of any port of that name when Europeans speak of it so freely must be conclusive.

The problem of the deltaic ports that looms so intricate as

one examines the maps of the early editions of Bernier, as one follows the location of Lahribandar now east and now west, now south, of Tatha, as again, bemused and bewildered, one attempts in vain to fix even the approximate position of duplicate names, is in fact the simpler one of deciding whether, after the foundation of Tatha, the ancient Debal survived in Tatha or in Lahribandar. And though it may be that there was no survival into the fourteenth century, but that Debal fell in the conflict of Sumrah and Sammah, if it survived the probabilities seem considerably stronger that it was Tatha than Lahribandar. To place much weight upon the details of Al-Beruni's account of the delta is perhaps rash, but the *Indika* mentions Lahribandar and Debal at the same time, and the distance given from the one to the other of twelve farsakhs is that which Manucci and Hamilton place between Sindi or Lahribandar and Tatha. But beyond this there is nothing in the location of Lahribandar near the Kohistan that suggests the sanctity of ancient Debal, whilst around the Makhli hills, contiguous to Tatha, there linger to-day traditions of Buddhist times, that still provide a *genius loci*, whilst their summit carries memories of a great temple[1] such as might have graced Debal.

[1] In his Progress Report, A.S.W.I., for the year ending 30 June, 1897, Mr. Cousens argues that Tatha is Debal because the tomb of Jam Nizamuddin at Tatha has been built from a Hindu temple which must have been of great magnificence. The original temple, he thinks, may have stood upon the plateau, or just below, at the old city of Samui.

VI

BAKHAR

BAKHAR

The eye of the forts and the face of the kingdom of Hind.

To define is to invite attack, and definitions of romance are many and various, but of a surety there is none that can quite rob Bakhar (Bukkur) of its claim to be the most romantic feature of the valley of Sind. In form not unsuggestive of Western build; reminiscent maybe of the Edwardian castle that bore the imprint of an Arab East as it broke upon the Crusaders; its position between the two towns of Sakhar (Sukkur) and Rorhi assisting to form a view that record has dwelt upon with pleasure for many a century. And more even than this, gathering around it that atmosphere of the elusive with all its charm, that attaches to so many sites of Sind, the origin of which persistently evades capture, its story is one that with no beginning opens in mystery. By chance or design again its proximity in name to Sakhar has furnished an alliterative jingle that, like some of the catchwords of Burton, has done more than sober recital of history to break down the seclusion of the lower Indus valley. At no other centre in the valley have the influences of desert and river so successfully combined to produce an atmosphere so lucent, and the unholy fascination of the unintelligible that dwells in the suggestions of desert sunset or the disturbing lure of the ephemeral beauty of opalescent hues that are too tender to last, are the gift of its air. And to this legend has added, in its name, associations of the dawn; for the name of the original settlement was traditionally changed to Ar-Bukr, when a holy *sayad* with the lowing of the cattle at dawn ('ar-bukr') came there to make his resting-place.[1]

[1] The *Tuhfat-ul Kiram* gives the earliest name of Bakhar as Ferista, and for the change of its name records 'They say that when Sayad Muhammad Makkyee arrived there it was in the morning ('ar-bukr') upon which he said, "Allah has ordained my morning in this blessed place." It is also related that before this, when the servants asked him where his abode should be fixed, he said, "Where you hear the cattle at sunrise ('ar-bukr')." After a time a change of pronunciation made the word Bukkur.' Inconsistent with itself, the same authority makes this Sayad leave Herat and Meshed in A.D. 1260, whereas in A.D. 1227 Nasiruddin Kabajah was besieged in Bakhar.

It would be hard to find in Sind a feature more explanatory of its history than is the fort of Bakhar. Traditionally the accidental successor to an Alor, ruined a few miles east by a legendary diversion of the river—a sequence falsified by the survival of Alor as a fort long after its decay as a town—its situation behind the desert of the north, its focus of the lines of invasion from Seistan and the upper reaches of the Indus, demonstrate unmistakably the strategic development of its position. From the eleventh century onwards the ancient highway of travel, immigration and invasion from Irak through Mekran, that made of the forts of lower Sind the first bulwarks against aggression, is superseded as a path of conquest, when the current of invasion sets in from further north; and the decay of Bahmanabad and Mansura,[1] however legend may surround their end, is a logical antecedent of the rise of Bakhar.

Exerting its influence throughout six centuries, the transfer of the strategic defence of Sind from its centre to the north is one of the main factors in the creation of that self-conscious separation in thought of upper and lower Sind, that finds expression to-day in the popular jest that a buffalo of the north is superior to a man of the south. It explains the curious independence of Debal until the last; the rise of the Sumrahs, and after them of the Sammahs, in the delta, and the comparative immunity of Tatha in its prime from aggression. It emphasizes the persisting inclination of the south to lead its life divorced from that of the rest of the valley, turning still southwards for its most intimate connections. A potential agent, in short, of unity, the chances of history have made its influence paramount in disruption. Its governors, as wardens of the marches, not infrequently attempt to carve out their own destiny; to the Jams of Tatha they are a problematic help or a nucleus of resistance in the contest of rival claimants to the throne of the south.[2]

[1] McMurdo thought that the rise of Bakhar was subsequent to the fall of Alor. Maj.-Gen. Haigh more accurately makes Bakhar supersede Mansura.

[2] Cf. Darya Khan's support of the minor Jam Feroz against rival claimants of Tatha. Equally resting upon possession of Bakhar is in 1555 the opposition of Sultan Muhammad Khan to Mirza Isa Tarkhan of Tatha, and in Bakhar is the nucleus of resistance to the hated rule of Mirza Muhammad Baku Tarkhan.

Now the history of Sind owes its somewhat amorphous monotony largely to the absence in its chronicle of any period of really unified rule; even in the short, brief day of Nasiruddin Kabajah or the more spacious days of the Mogul there is no real unity; the north is always there ready to break away from the south, and the existence of Bakhar, strange to say, is indirectly one of the prime influences that have operated to deny to Sind the advantage of a central rule. It was not as this that Sind history gave early promise. In the reigns of its Brahman rulers, who were before the Arab invasion, Sind looked westward for an extension of its sovereignty, with the usual tendency of all empires to extend in the direction of the greatest pressure; from the same west came the first invasion of Islam, and it is no fortuitous chance that around Bahmanabad and Mansura there grew up a semblance of unified sovereignty. In the days before the Ghaznis, the dangers of the door, that near the sea over the low passes lay open to the invader, produced a unity within the valley which disappeared when it fell to one half to be its defender, and to the other to forget in comparative peace the lessons of the past. *Ex parvo multum:* from the redirection of the current of invasion follow in sequence the record of petty strife; the many failures to achieve unity that render the reading of Sind history unattractive; follows, too, the existing cleavage between the north and south of Sind; follows, in fact, the supreme influence for good and evil of the unique position of Bakhar.

In a manner almost traditional to the treatment of Sind history, conjecture has paid homage with no stint to the externals of that position. Tod, adding to his many erroneous sketches of Sind, described the river as near a mile wide on either side of Bakhar; with an unbridled enthusiasm characteristic of his age for traces of the great Alexander, he found the 'islandic Bekher' in the pages of Arrian, and then with happy forgetfulness of logic traced in the same fort the lineaments of the eighth century Arab fortress of Mansura. The traditions of its impregnability indeed, and the seeming permanence of its surroundings, were without a doubt the cause of these and other similar errors, that were consistent only in declining to recognise in a situation so unique a creation that did not of necessity possess a hoary past, and this building up of a theory upon little more than semblances is illustrated most clearly in Pottinger's etymological discovery that the Arabic 'Mansur', as meaning 'defended' or 'victorious', must bear reference to the peculiar strength of the Bakhar stronghold.[1]

It is not, however, solely as a fort that the interest of Bakhar claims attention, for hardly less than this is its interest as a town, connected in a way that is not over clear with the town of Sakhar. Its first[2] recorded appearance in the time of Nasiruddin Kabajah reveals a town with one fort and possibly even two forts upon a peninsula; it is still a town of Bakhar that with its suburbs Shah Hassein Arghun (1528) surrounds with a wall, and a fortified town that resists successfully the emperor Humayun. From A.D. 1572 onwards, however, the name of Sakhar introduces a new problem, and the confusion of the two names henceforward suggests that the latter is nothing more than an alliterative of Bakhar, consequent upon the division of the fort from the town by the river Indus.[3]

Mandelslo and Sir Thomas Roe both speak of a single city striding the river—the former's Backarhukon, the latter's Buckar-Suckar—and priority in name is given to Bakhar. Others, beginning with Salbanke in 1609 and ending with Kennedy in the last century, transpose the names, giving that of Sakhar to the island fort. Withington mentions Bakhar alone, whilst McMurdo in 1833 makes Seiggar a suburb of Bhakir, thus

[1] Pottinger found in Bakhar the capital of the Sogdi, though, as Postans and Burton remarked, if this were so it would be hard to explain the silence of the Greek historians as to any such geographical feature. Abu Fazl found Mansura in Bakhar, and bequeathed another error for Tiffentheler, Vincent, Rennell, Tod, and Pottinger to follow.

[2] The *Gazetteer of Sind* writes of a Sheikh Abu Turab, whose tomb bears the date of A.D. 788, as having taken the fortress of Bukkur. It is impossible to believe that this can refer to the Bakhar that is the subject of this essay. Bakhar played no part either in the invasion or in the occupation of Sind by the Arabs, and neither the *Chachnama* nor the Arab authorities allude to it. Had it existed at this time it must have played a very important part.

[3] Bakhar is not mentioned in the *Chachnama*, the early chronicles of the Arab conquest, nor is it alluded to in the time of the Ghaznivide Sultans. From the early thirteenth century Bakhar is a familiar name. In the reign of Akbar it is the capital of a province of the same name. Mir Ma'asumi speaks of the villages and towns of Bakhar. Even up to 1815 it gives a name to a province of Multan (*vide East India Gazetteer* of Hamilton). 'Buckar, through whose capital city, called Suckor, the noble Indus makes its way' (Terry). Neither Mandelslo nor Sir Thomas Herbert mentions Sakhar.

bringing up to the nineteenth century the subordination of Sakhar and the importance of the name Bakhar.

The origin of Sakhar, as is that of Bakhar, is an unsolved question, but it would seem beyond doubt that its appearance coincides with some division of the ancient Bakhar. The *Ain-i-Akbari* does not mention Sakhar, nor does the *Tarikh-i-Ma'asumi* in relating the siege of Bakhar by Humayun, but thirty years later Akbar enjoins the division of the governorship of Bakhar and Sakhar, and a bipartite or tripartite division of this military charge remains until in 1585 the whole is held as a *jagir* holding. When, however, the fort was definitely severed from the town it is impossible to say. Only in the last century the branch of the river that passes Bakhar on the west was artificially widened, and McMurdo wrote of its waters disappearing entirely during the dry season. And so, even if Ibn Batuta (1333) describes Bakhar as a handsome city divided by an arm of the Indus, one need not assume even more than a seasonal division, for even to-day the river craft moving south invariably take the eastern channel, those going north with human labour against the stream equally invariably taking the western course.

Apart, too, from the still existing features of the western branch of the river adjoining the island of Bakhar, it is easy to mark with some assurance changes in the size of the island itself, for in 1658 Manucci gives a detailed account of the island fort, wherein he commanded the artillery on behalf of Dara Shukoh. He writes that the seven rivers only touched its sides for a pistol shot on the west and two musket shots on the east; describes, too, sallies from the fort by the garrison, which resulted in the capture of the enemy's field-pieces, and gives for the island dimensions[1] that, particularly in breadth, are much greater than those given by Kennedy two hundred years subsequently. The slow and gradual formation of the insular position of Bakhar is certain; uncertainty attaches only to the riddle of its name and that of Sakhar.

[1] Manucci says the length of the island is 975 paces and its breadth 553. Kennedy gives the length and breadth as respectively 800 and 300 yards.

In the time of Humayun the fort did not cover the island, for there was fighting between the walls of the fort and the river.

Bakhar-Sakhar, what is their secret? In the thirteenth century Akar and Bakhar are names of two forts attributed to the islands or peninsulas of the Indus.[1] From alliteration thus through alliteration, for Mandelslo's Backarhukon and Sir Thomas Roe's Buckar-Suckar seem but this, these names come down. The first is no uncommon name even in Sind; the second, as a name for a riverain port, has gained its seniority slowly, though it began its issue with Bakhar four hundred years ago. For centuries the constant objective of treaty[2] yet not the actual spoil of conquest; the defender of the valley yet a factor making for disunion; withal its beginning shrouded in obscurity, its life chequered with the interest that accompanies all great change, Bakhar, 'the eye of the forts, and the face of the kingdom of Hind,' has surrendered, victim of physical changes beyond its control, its birthright to another, and an alliterative jingle rather than a recollection of its eventful history may yet become its best preserver against the fate that overtakes the ancient memorials of Sind.

[1] 'Akar and Bakhar, two forts on an island' (*Jahan Kushao*). 'Akar and Bakhar, two forts on two "jazirahs"' (*Jami'ul-Tawarikh*). Speaking of the same events, namely the investment of Nasiruddin Kabajah, the *Jami'ul Hikayat* and the *Taj-ul-Maasir* speak of one fort only.

[2] The *Tarkhan-nama* says that Shah Beg laid out the town of Bakhar in quarters for his troops; that he had a plan of the town made; that he destroyed the fort of Alor for bricks to repair Bakhar, destroying also the houses of some of the residents in the suburbs of Bakhar. Mir Ma'asumi adds that the Sayads were turned out of Bakhar and given ground in Rorhi.

When Bakhar springs upon us it had a reputation throughout India for being impregnable and for having never been conquered. There is no record of a successful assault of the fort under the governors appointed by the Ghazni Ghor or the Taghlak kings of Delhi. Shah Beg Arghun obtained it by treaty after the capture of Tatha, and in his time it witnessed many a siege. The Dharejahs tried in vain to take it from the Sayads. In 1540 Sultan Muhammad Khan held it successfully against Humayun. It was unassailable for centuries, and this though its position was not insular as now.

VII

TATHA

TATHA

On its alluvial levels, guarded from the river by dykes, Tatha is to-day an ordinary Sindhi town with little claim to attention, save when the heat haze shrouds its angular form, and from the waste that lies between it and the hills, it appears in the distance like a fairy city of white not far removed from the deceit of mirage. But behind the town and further from the river runs a low range of hills, at one time a coast-line of the delta, whereon amid scrub and ruin rise the tombs and mosques of older settlements, for Tatha has the interest of towns that, like Laon and Carcassone, have stepped down from their heights to humbler levels, that like the Rhine of Victor Hugo have descended *des idées hautes aux idées larges*, and despite all the possible advantages of their new position have forfeited for ever the distinction of primal nobility.

Among the interesting sites of the valley Tatha has an interest quite its own. Though geographical considerations alone make impossible any revival of its claim to be the Patala of the Greek historians; though, too, its lineal descent from Debal be still unproved, it is from the fourteenth century onwards the sole centre of real history in the valley. Its days of glory explain the attraction that drew the imperial adventurers of the East India Company; they explain the European view of Sind in the seventeenth and eighteenth centuries as an El Dorado and Utopia of wealth beyond avarice; and contrariwise its chequered fortunes illustrate the factors that have created an advancing delta, and give reason for those melancholy traditions of half a century that culminated in making the valley notorious as 'The Unhappy Valley'.

On the hills of Tatha is the tomb of an unknown Englishman: one Edward Cooke, who died there in 1743; his tomb, erected by servants, is aligned as the graves of good Moslems. It is a reminder that British connection with Sind is one extending far beyond the last century, and a corrective of those ideas that make Sind a closed book to Europe before its strategic position as an approach to Afghanistan brought it into the field of international politics. It is too often forgotten that the relations of the East India Company with Sind cover a century and a half; that the Company's factors were stationed in several towns even north of the delta, and that the trade routes of the valley were more familiar to the Company's agents of the seventeenth century than they were to the 'politicals' of the nineteenth century.[1] The ports of the delta; the river route from Lahore to the sea; even the desert route by Jasalmir, were all explored in the seventeenth century, and though the maps of this century may be full of strange duplications and confusions, the errors of understanding are not errors in the laconic reports of the Company's agents.

To the trader or traveller from the West in these earlier centuries Sind was, practically speaking, synonymous with Tatha.[2] The first instructions given by the Company with respect to the extension of its activities in Sind were those issued to its captains in 1607 to sail to 'Laurie, a good harbour within two miles of Negartuttie, a great city as big as London' (and London had then a population of two hundred thousand souls). A few years later, 1613, Captain Paynton landed at Diul, and wrote of Tatha as one of the most celebrated marts of India. The beginning of a factory was made at Tatha in 1635; the English welcomed there their Dutch rivals in 1652, and both Tavernier and Manucci found English factories in the delta.

It is now hard, from the depressing scene of the delta of to-day, to imagine the Tatha of the seventeenth century, or those surroundings of fertility that provoked the superlative rhetoric of successive travellers. Terry, the chaplain of Sir Thomas Roe, spoke of the valley as 'very fruitful and pleasant . . . rich and fertile almost as covetousness could wish,' and the islands below Tatha were a common theme. Mandelslo, borrowing from others, praised the artisans[3] of

[1] Cf. the *Gazetteer of Sind*, which, in a paragraph headed 'The Beginning of British Intercourse with Sind,' remarks that at the beginning of the nineteenth century Sind was an almost unknown country to the English, and that in 1758 the East India Company founded a factory at Tatha.

[2] Sir Thomas Herbert put Tatha east of Jasalmir and west from 'Buckor'. Bernier, or rather the maps that accompany the earlier editions, have a confusion of Tatha and Bakhar.

[3] 'The finest Pallanquins in India are made at Tatha, and there is nothing neater and more convenient than the chariots made here, but their waggon wheels are one piece of solid timber like a mill stone' (Tavernier).

Tatha as the most industrious in the kingdom of the Moghul; Thevenot described the town as one of the most commodious in India though exceeding hot, and Tavernier classed it as one of the greatest cities of India. At this time forty thousand vessels[1] plied for hire at Tatha as the port of the Indus traffic. Famous, too, for learning, theology, politics and philology, we still read of her a century later as possessing more than four hundred colleges.

But this glory of Tatha was for a few centuries only. Already in the time of Thevenot and Tavernier the river had been silting up, and the trade from Agra and the north, that had met the river at Bakhar, was going south directly to Surat by land. Its port of Lahribandar was already, at the beginning of the seventeenth century, some fourteen miles from the sea, and communication by water with Tatha became increasingly difficult; the *Tarikh-i-Tahiri* speaks of such communication being made by an unfordable channel but a small one; Fremlen and others refer to the dangerous bar at the mouth of the river, whilst Spiller, in 1646, reports that the tide reaches only halfway to Tatha, involving the necessity of drawing boats by sheer strength on poles through water in places not more than a foot deep. Aurangzeb attempted to open a new port, which Spiller and Scrivener (1652) name Cuckerhallah, but the decay of Tatha could not be arrested nor, as Thevenot relates, the associated decay of Lahore and Multan, in consequence of the damage done to their trade by the extra cost of taking goods by land to Surat.

By the early forties of the last century the romance of Tatha was quite at an end. Pottinger found long streets of uninhabited houses and a population overrated at twenty thousand souls, but the town he still found six miles in circumference, exclusive of the ruins. Hamilton found its fortified wall and towers a heap of ruins. Kennedy described it still more depressingly as a collection of mud-built hovels with a scanty population of two thousand, and Postans found its glory 'completely departed' and its appearance 'ruined and deserted'.

Its ruins, however, gave it a fame even in the nineteenth century, and became a common subject of sentimental brooding

[1] The exaggeration of a Sammah historian must be discounted.

. . . those 'cities of the dead and the cemetery of six square miles, that contain not less than a million tombs,' as Kennedy wrote in 1838, '. . . a Mecca of Indian Moslems,' as Ross erroneously imagined the name of the hills suggested.[1]

Yet withal this, the memories of Tatha are more pregnant than the memories of a city that has fallen, for they are those of a complete history gone beyond recall. The story of Tatha is the last page in the record of what will always be the supreme interest of Sind history, lifting her annals above the monotone of anonymity—the history of the Indus delta—for last in succession of ports and emporia that gave Sind a place among the nations, and postulated a wealth that attracted the recurrent cupidity of the West, her end is the winding up that ends a tale for ever. The nineteenth century could brood with sentimental lament over the departed glory of Tatha, but a greater knowledge of the destructive play of geographical forces, in the accretions of the delta, allows realisation that with the decay of Tatha the continuity of a tale has been lost beyond retrieve.

The very names of the ports and deltaic capitals that were before Tatha are a vivid and varied testimony to the historic wealth of the delta. Patala, if it cannot be taken as one of the earliest Aryan settlements in India, recalls at least the voyage of discovery made by Skylax, and the Greek invasion of the Indus valley, which were to capture for Greece the Sabæan trade that carried the products of Arabia and India to the heads of the Red Sea and the Persian Gulf. Tiyu and Taiz invoke visions of that coasting trade[2] that linked Canton with the Persian Gulf, as Barbarei is a reminder of the overland route that, across the dark Karakoram, connected Cathay with the ports of the Indus. And yet even more than this, from the ports of the delta sailed maybe the Sumerians,[3] whom we first find in the fourth millennium B.C. as a civilised power in

[1] 'Makli literally means Little Mecca' (Ross).
'The hill (Makli) takes its name from the occupant of one of the earlier tombs—a woman called Makli' (H. Cousens).

[2] The *Itinerary of Kia Tan*, compiled between A.D. 785 and 805, defines the sea route between Canton and the Persian Gulf (*vide* Hirth Rockhill, *Chau-Ju Kua*).

[3] *The Ancient History of the Near East*, by H. R. Hall. The author puts forward the theory that the Sumerians were an Indian non-Aryan race, and

Babylonia. A lodestar always, the delta of the Indus. Sumerian; Sabæan; Greek; last, but not least, the East India Company of the seventeenth century; a sequence of adventure. Of old a land of fabled wealth,[1] the delta has buried its past—Patala, Barbarei, Tiyu, Debal lie lost beyond retracing. Tatha survives, but she is divorced completely from the history of the delta, for the river, remorseless in its creative task, has shaped its end.

possibly from the Indus valley. He opines that the legend of Oannes the Man-Fish, quoted by Berossus, argues an early marine connection of Babylonia with a civilised land oversea, and that the Sumerians passed from the Indus valley to that of the two rivers both by sea and by land.

[1] The Ophir of the Scriptures has been placed in Sind. It matters not with what accuracy.

VIII

THE ALOR BUND

THE ALOR BUND

The story of the merchant who, to save a threatened maid from the hands of a Hindu ruler of Alor,[1] the one-time capital of Sind, constructed a dam which changed the course of the river, enabling him to sail past the barrier[2] at Alor, is the most familiar of Sind legends. It has never, indeed, lacked its defenders. Accepting literally its details, the nineteenth

[1] Alor is identified tentatively with the capital of Mousikanos by Dr. Vincent Smith, who also makes it the P'i-shan-p'o-pu-lo of Hiuen Tsang.

Cunningham wrote that the original name was probably Rora and that the initial vowel was derived from the Arabic prefix 'Al', that in Hindi this word signifies 'noise', 'roar', and also fame, and that therefore the full name of the city may have been Rorapura or Roranagara, i.e. the 'Famous city'. Raverty says the derivation of 'Rurhi' is from 'rur', in reference to its situation on the rocky limestone ridge, and the significance of which is 'rough', 'stiff', 'rugged', and that there is another word, 'rora', signifying 'stone', 'rock'. He points out that the 'Al' has nothing to do with the Arabic prefix, as the name was written Alor and Aror before the Arabs came to Sind.

Typical of the identifications of the last century is Tod's happy discovery of this city on the island of Bakhar.

[2] 'Below the city of Alor or Aror the river constituting the Panj Ab flowed, which is likewise called Hakra, Wahindah and Wahan indiscriminately, which sends its waters into the great sea. Dilu Rao governed the territory between Alor and Muhammad Tur. From the merchants who brought their merchandise by the river from Hind, on their way to the port of Dewal, he levied one-half as toll.' After the demand for the merchant's handmaiden and the grant of three days' grace to the merchant, the *Tarikh-i-Tahiri* continues: 'During this period he collected a number of skilled men, who in the piercing of mountains exceeded the renowned Farhad and were able to close a breach in a rampart like that of the Sadd-i-Sikandar. He bestowed on these men whatever they desired, gold, gems, valuable cloths, and the like, his object being to throw up a strong embankment on the river above Alor and divert the waters in the direction of Bakhar. Night after night these strong workmen laboured to excavate a fresh channel and throw up an embankment, and thereby turned the river aside towards Sehwan and the Lakhhi hills, and with such force that the merchant through God's mercy was speedily carried away beyond the reach of the tyrannical raja.'

'Saif-ul-Mulk is the name of a great and rich merchant, who in the early part of the fourth century of the Hijrat brought about the ruin of Alor. The tract of country then dependent on it was ruled by a raja—for the power of the Musalmans had waxed weak in these parts at that time—who was called Dilu Rao, who was a great tyrant and deflowerer of maidens. The merchant arrived near Alor with his merchandise, which was of great value, laden in vessels on the river, which was then navigable from a great distance upwards, down to the great ocean, and he had also with him a beautiful handmaiden, named Badil-ul-Jamal. Not content with plundering the merchant of a considerable portion of his goods, the raja also demanded that the handmaiden should be given up to him. Finding what a tyrant he had to deal with, the merchant resolved with God's help to make a bold endeavour to escape from him. He

century made several identifications of the embankment[1] with the same comfortable assurance with which it interpreted the traditions of Alexander, and even the failure of Lieutenant Fife, specially deputed to find the dam, to trace any such construction, did not deter a later advocate from maintaining the truth of the original account. To-day a scepticism that smiles at its picturesque incidents accepts generally its story as an undisciplined effort to explain the westering of the Indus; as, in fact, a substitute for an unadorned statement of Baer's law, whilst it would be a breach with orthodoxy to dissociate it entirely from the formation of the Bakhar gorge.

Now the story itself has been added to and changed from time to time. As it first appears, the merchant has no particular

asked to be allowed three days' grace—some say eight days—after which he would comply with the demands made upon him and deliver up the damsel. In the meantime, by means of his wealth having got together a number of artisans and numerous labourers, he set to work day and night to raise a great bând, or dyke, upstream above Alor, and by making a new channel to divert the waters of the Hakra or Wahud farther westward towards Bakhar. This diversion he effected; and on awaking in the morning of the day on which the days of grace expired, instead of a broad and deep river running near Alor, what did the tyrant discover but its bed full of mud and some muddy water. The river had left it and was running towards Siwistan and the Lakhhi hills, and the merchant and his vessels had been wafted thereon far beyond his reach, and Alor ruined.'

[1] Sir Alexander Burnes found the dam in the remains of a masonry bridge over a canal near Alor. Rathborne reported his information acquired, of a dam two miles broad with an average thickness of fifty yards. Inverarity thought he had found it in one six hundred feet long with a height of twenty-two feet.

The most detailed defence is that of Major Raverty (*vide Journal R. Asiatic Society Bengal*, 1892). He relies largely upon two dates—the one of Al Masudi, the other a date of an inscription in the shrine of Khwajah Khizr. Al Masudi is interpreted to indicate that Alor in his days was on the western bank of the river. Now Al Masudi's description of Sind is not without its difficulties. His knowledge of Alor and of the river below Alor is weak. He gives no description of Alor; he wrongly places at Alor a bifurcation of the river which all other authorities put near Mansuriyah; he mentions none of the places between Alor and Mansuriyah that are familiar in other writings, and omits a division of the river near Mansuriyah. It seems dangerous to make his description of Alor as on the west of the river the basis of a theory.

As for the Persian inscription in the shrine, this is to the effect that the shrine was encircled by the river in A.D. 962.

'Know that when this fabric was raised
Khizr's waters encompassed it around
This pleasing hemistich Khizr wrote
In the "Court of God" the date is found.'

Or as Maj.-Gen. Haigh translated it:—

'When this sublime temple appeared
Which is surrounded by the waters of Khizr.'

Unfortunately, the Archæological Department regards the inscription as a late addition, and the Sindhi himself smiles at it as a pious fraud contrived to give the shrine a hoary antiquity.

name, but is one of those who passed for trade from the upper reaches of the Indus to Debal. In the eighteenth century he is given the name of Saif-ul-Mulk, and is represented as going on a pilgrimage to Mecca. Finally, a modern version of the legend calls him Shah Hassein, and attributes the diversion of the river not to any embankment, the work of human hands, but to the miraculous interposition of Khwajah Khizr, who on the merchant's repeated prayers, draws the river with its burden of boats away from the vicinity of Alor. There is thus a gradual enlargement of the story, until it becomes a pretty story of poetic justice vindicating the virtues of Islam, and in its latest form attesting the ancient origin of an existing shrine.

The original source of the story is unknown, as our first authority to mention it does not declare its sources. It receives no support from early writers. The translator of the *Chachnama* has nothing to say about any such change in the river's course, though he visited the vicinity of Alor in A.D. 1216; even the *Tarikh-i-Ma'asumi* does not allude to the story, though we are told that in his passion for inscriptions its author placed inscribed stones in the bed of the diverted river. Yet, again, none of the writers first to speak about Bakhar have any allusion to the Alor legend, though the peninsular and eventual insular position of Bakhar are supposed to have followed from the diversion of the river from near Alor. Sind record, indeed, is peculiarly innocent of legend until the rise of the historians of

Finally Major Raverty interprets a passage of the *Tarikh-i-Ma'asumi* so as to make the emperor Akbar, on the dissent of his ministers, revoke an order posting Tarsun Muhammad Khan to Bakhar, because forsooth of the danger of placing at this frontier post a descendant of Saif-ul-Mulk. The story as we have it from this date does not in fact bear the name of the merchant, and in any case the impropriety of placing at Bakhar, as guardian of the marches, a descendant of a merchant who had vindicated Islam six hundred years before is not apparent. It is improbable, too, that Mir Ma'asumi would make this allusion to the story and no more. According to the *Ain-i-Akbari*, Tarsun Khan was actually appointed jagirdar of Bakhar, and his uncle, Saif-ul-Mulk, had been an independent ruler in Gurjistan, quite recently put down by Tahmasp. This would be a better reason for the dissent of the ministers than the one suggested by Major Raverty in support of his theory.

According to tradition, the Alor Bund is to be burst again and the Hakra become once more a perennial stream.

> 'Dyke of Alor be burst, and flow
> Hakro perennial to the main;
> Swim ye fish, ye lilies grow
> Where Sammahs plough the sultry plain.'

Tatha; there is little departure from sober recital in the *Chachnama*, and the Arab records are difficult of interpretation by reason of their cryptic brevity. With the *Tarikh-i-Tahiri* completed in A.D. 1606, however, begins the submerging of history in fictitious incident and its colouring by a melodramatic relation of the conflict between Sumrah and Sammah. The legends of the Tatha school of historians dominate the popular history of to-day, and in making headway against the meretricious attraction of their simplicity historic truth has a task of much difficulty.

In detail there is not a single important element in this original story of the Alor Bund that is not contradicted by events subsequent to any of the dates attributed to this legendary change in the river's course. For that change is represented as taking the river towards Bakhar, as leading to the prosperity of western Sind and the dessication of eastern Sind; as above all leading to the immediate ruin of Alor; yet not one of these consequences of the action of the merchant is testified to by any evidence that we can accept.

As to the immediate ruin of a city which early writers describe as being as large as Multan, there is no evidence to show that it was abandoned suddenly, either by the river or by its inhabitants. Arab record[1] of writers who for the greater part visited Sind consistently shows Alor as near the river up to the thirteenth century, and, still more than this, long after any of the dates assigned to the diversion, describes in detail the same as before the course of the river below Alor to Mansura.

Equally emphatic is the testimony to the survival as a place of importance[2] of the city alleged to have been destroyed by sudden catastrophe. The translator of the *Chachnama* presumably did not find a ruined city in A.D. 1216: Al Beruni

[1] Al Masudi (A.D. 942) puts Alror, Aldor, on the western bank. The *Istakhari* (A.D. 951-61) describes Alor as near the Mihran. Ibn Haukal (A.D. 976) says the Mihran passes Alor. Al Beruni says the waters bend to the west from the city of Alor. Al Idrisi writes of Dor as on the bank of the Mihran, which flows west of that city. The map of Ashkal-ul-Bilad puts Alror on the bank.

[2] The *Tarikh-i-Ma'asumi* speaks, too, of the tripartite governorship of Sakhar, Bakhar and Alor, and of the governor of Mathelo becoming the governor of Alor. The *Ain-i-Akbari* gives Alor as a mahal of the sarkar of Bakhar, with a revenue of 1,132,150 dams, and as supplying 200 cavalry and 500 infantry; as possessing a fort and occupied by Dharejahs.

speaks of the city of Alor; the *Tarikh-i-Ma'asumi* writes of Alor and its fort and describes Rorhi as near Alor; whilst the *Ain-i-Akbari* alludes to its fort and details the contingent of foot and horse, and the revenue obtained from the district of which it was the centre. It is significant, too, that the Arorahs, a caste of Hindus still existing in Shikarpur, witness to the former wealth of Alor, have no tradition among themselves as to the cause which made them leave Alor.

Casting aside *a priori* assumptions creating a bias in interpretation, the Arab record itself permits of another explanation of the river's courses in the eighth to the twelfth centuries. Our Arab authorities and maps clearly indicate an important trade route between Alor and Mansura east of the river, with trade centres at a distance from the river. Between Alor and the bifurcation of the river, forty miles north of Mansura, there is not a single town shown as on the bank of the river. In other words, there is here ample proof that between Alor and Mansura was no dessicated territory, still less a belt of ruined country extending into the delta as far as Muhammad Tur. The survival of Mansura also makes absurd in the extreme the account of the *Tarikh-i-Tahiri*.[1]

There remains the evidence of the *Chachnama*, which in its account of the campaigns of Chach, and again of the Arab general, lends no support to the theory that Alor was on the western bank of a single stream. In their marches north of Alor, both Chach and Muhammad Kasim reach the Biah, but of neither is it said that from Alor he had to cross the river to reach the eastern bank on which he was when he reached the Biah. Similarly, Chach, marching south-west from Alor, crossed the river at Dahiyat, a crossing inexplicable if Alor was already on

[1] 'From the year of the Hijri 700 until 843 . . . the Hindu tribe of Sumra were the rulers of Sind; and that portion which is now flourishing was then a mere waste owing to the scarcity of water in the Sind or Panj Ab river, which is known by the above name below Bakhar. No water flowed towards those regions. . . . The capital of this people was the city of Muhammad Tur, which is now depopulated and is included in the pergana of Dirak. Not I alone, but many others, have beheld these ruins with astonishment. . . . The cause of the ruins of that above-named city and of its dependencies, which had flourished between 900 and 1,000 years, was as follows: Dilu Rao governed the country between Muhammad Tur and Alor. . . .

'The people of Sumra, who occupied the city of Muhammad Tur, and its vicinity, where ruin had followed the erection of the bând of Alor . . .'

the west of the river, and the Arabs, coming up the river from Bahmanabad, which was to the east of the river, do not seem to have had to make a crossing to the west of the river to attain Alor. Yet another point with reference to the evidence of the *Chachnama*: this authority mentions a river Kunbh as flowing between the Mihran and Sehwan, and this no chance wandering of the Ab-i-Sind or Mihran, for it was the boundary of the Budiyah territory and bore on its banks several towns and Buddhist temples. .

Our authorities, therefore, most definitely do not assist an assumption that the river was suddenly diverted from east to west of Alor between the eighth and eleventh centuries, but, on the contrary, there is some reason for thinking that even in these centuries there was a branch of the Mihran flowing through the Alor cleft west of Alor, and that the modern Eastern Nara channel, so far from having been one of the earliest courses of the Hakra, was in its upper reaches one of its later ones.

The association of a river diverted from the vicinity of Alor with the formation of the Bakhar gorge is the accepted conjecture that makes difficult the suggestion of such a new aspect. Yet even the legendary accounts of the Alor story do not attribute to the merchant the formation of the gorge, and no single authority alludes to the forces that created the position of Bakhar, which acquired so unique a reputation throughout India. The association is, in short, a theory of the last century, and, like that century's settlement of many problems of the Alexandrian traditions, speciously simple in its premises, for it rests on nothing more than the dried-up state of the Eastern Nara as we then found it, and a simplification of the river's former courses. To suppose that after the Arab invasion the river began to flow towards Sehwan is to forget the ancient history of Sehwan; to assume a diversion creating the position of Bakhar leaves unexplained the failure of three centuries to seize upon its strategic importance; to predicate a western Sind suddenly sharing in the bounty of the river neglects the evidence that western Sind at the time of the Arab invasion was covered with marsh and lake, and watered by tributaries that joined the Mihran from the border hills. Break with the interpretations of the nineteenth century, and it is even easier to believe that the Bakhar gorge was formed by waters that came from the west of Sind than it is to think that it followed a capricious change in eastern Sind.

It remains to offer some rational explanation of a legend which cannot be dismissed altogether as a happy piece of fiction. To suggest that it is an effort to explain a westering river only raises the further question, why any one particular change out of the countless changes in the river's course should have been singled out by legend, and why sober historical record should remain so persistently silent about it. It is surely more probable that a capricious river was the *deus ex machina* of Sind legend, and of that history that subordinates truth to political and religious prejudice; a simple solution to offer of any problem that might be troublesome to an historical conscience.

The moral stories of the iniquity of Dilu Rao; the earthquakes and divine visitations that have dotted the valley with many a Sodom and Gomorrah,[1] are as surely the confession of Islam in defeat as the melodramatic history of the Sumrahs conceals the chagrin of orthodoxy in decline. There are two factors making for the falsification of Sind history, for there is the Karmatian heresy, brought into the valley by the Sumrah port of Debal, and the revolt of Hinduism against the rule of Islam, and as the dates of these synchronise, the result is a studied fabrication or concealment of incident that gives to Sind its dark age of several centuries. Roughly measured from the tenth to the thirteenth centuries, Sind history is fiction masquerading in poor disguise; in these centuries there is the mystery that attends the fall of Bahmanabad, the disappearance of Mansura, the ruin of Alor; the mystery of the rise of Bakhar and that which hangs around the dynasty of the Sumrahs. And beyond these questions that Sind record raises without answer, there are questions that outside record suggest: why do the records of the Solanki kings of Anhilawada

[1] The legend of Dilu Rao is attached to many a ruined site in Sind. Mounds of this king are common around Mansura. The idea of moral obliquity connected with earthquake is common in India. Ibn Batuta found the remains of a wicked city in the delta.

testify to a long struggle with overlords of Sind, to which Sind record has not the slightest allusion, and why are these centuries marked by so many migrations from Sind?

The persistent intrusion of legendary fiction in the account of these centuries permits a conjecture that the legend of Alor is nothing more than a picturesque attempt to conceal a failure of Islam, following closely upon the lines of the story that would explain the ruin of Bahmanabad.[1]

In this respect it is singular that the record of the Solanki princes of Anhilawada, the *Dvaiasharaya*, a Hindu work completed in A.D. 1225, affords a curious parallel to the legend of Alor. The Solanki, Bhim, is said to have invaded Sind in the eleventh century and subdued a powerful overlord of the valley, who had roused the anger of Bhim by the composition of insulting books. The moon-descended prince thereupon marched to where the five rivers of the Panj Ab met to form a single stream, and there broke down the bulwark of the Sind raja by diverting the river. This he accomplished by breaking down hills with great stones and constructing a bridge, which even before it was completed changed the course of the river and enabled the invader to cross and conquer the Sind ruler. Even as the merchant of the Alor story spurred on his men by the gift of everything they desired, so the prince encouraged his army to superhuman effort by the distribution of luxuries—a similarity of detail that makes the parallel still more close and interesting. There are thus two distinct stories as to the diversion of the river in upper Sind; the one from the records of Gujarat and of the thirteenth century, the other of the seventeenth century, but of unknown source, given us by the historians of Tatha. Is it too much to think that the stories relate to the same event and preserve the memory of some change in the river's course of the twelfth century, which

[1] Mr. H. Cousens opines that Mansura was overthrown by a Hindu revolt (*Vide Progress Reports of the Archæological Survey of Western India*, 1895-1897). It was sacked and the Muhammadan historians were ashamed to chronicle such downfall at the hands of idolaters. All valuables were carried away; skeletons huddled together and on thresholds indicate massacre; scattered beads indicate force. If the town had been gradually deserted people would have taken away even their copper coins. And why desert it? They could have dug wells. *Idem passim.* Archæology, therefore, definitely refutes one theory of earthquake.

legend subsequently seized upon with avidity as explanation of a defeat of Islam, and solemnly accepted without any consideration of date. It is at least quite clear that the *Tarikh-i-Tahiri* does not know in what century to put its occurrence, and finds it a convenient explanation of incidents in no wise connected historically, to wit, the fall of Alor, the ruin of Bahmanabad, the defeat of the Sumrahs—events which together cover a period of some four centuries, according to its own computation of dates.

IX

THE SUMRAHS

THE SUMRAHS

If to be without history is a prelude to a country's happiness, Sind has in very truth laboured hard to win the proverbial reward of self-effacement, for her historical record is a complete reversal in its sequences of the stages through which the evolution of a country's annals ordinarily proceeds. In lieu of a story that advances from fiction to fact, in progress from undisciplined indulgence to studied sobriety; in lieu of a history that throws off gradually the accompaniments of folk-lore and myth with which it first appeared, Sind record, from the cryptic and pregnant severity of Arab record, breaks forth in the seventeenth and eighteenth centuries into a riot of extravagant absurdities and unhistorical accretions, which still remain the basis of the history of the valley as it is popularly accepted to-day. Nor is it less strange that, as if realising the gap that separates these later centuries from the days of the Arab occupation, the broken collation that is given in explanation of five centuries of darkness conceals entirely the sources of its origin.

The question of a Sumrah overlordship of Sind is one of those problems of which attempted solution has passed from one extreme to the other. From acceptance by Tod of the statement of Ferishta and the *Ain-i-Akbari* that the Sumrah dynasty followed in strict succession that of the *Tamin-i-Ansari*, to the conclusion of Elliot that the Sumrahs could have been a dynasty by virtue only of the absence of serious rivals, answers to the question have passed from confident affirmation to sceptical indifference, and as one of a number of unimportant warring tribes the Sumrahs are now usually dismissed with little consideration. Their connection, however, with the Karmatian heresy, which came into Sind by the Sumrah port of Debal, which in the eleventh century had its stronghold at Mansura and a leader in a Sumrah chief, forbids so hasty a rejection of the evidence of a Sumrah overlordship.

The connection of the Sumrahs with this heresy is apparent in the garbled account of their rule given by the writers of the seventeenth and eighteenth centuries. The *Tarikh-i-Tahiri*, written by a Sammah historian of Tatha; the *Tuhfat-ul-Kiram*, indebted to the former and also written by a historian of Tatha, betray the virulent animosity of orthodoxy against heresy. By the former the Sumrahs are represented as below the average man in intelligence; by the latter as above him in arrogance and vice; to the example of the Sumrahs is attributed, without any attention to the propriety of dates, the vices of the semi-mythical Dilu Rao, who brought about the ruin of Alor and Bahmanabad; it is their vices again that bring in the armies of Delhi in retribution, and it is as Evil incarnate that their destruction is complete. In the melodramatic account that makes even the womenfolk of the Sumrahs in retreat swallowed up by a mountain so that the race might end; that makes the cities of the Sumrahs accursed and their fields for ever left uncultivated; that brings in the moral stories of the Alor Bund and of the destruction of Bahmanabad to illustrate the wrath of heaven; in all this is evidence enough to demonstrate the bitterness of sectarian difference and the intolerance of proselytism. And yet even more significant is the emphasis of the Utopian peace that the Sammahs introduced, and the rapid progress that orthodoxy made under their ægis.

It is impossible, therefore, to expect from Sindhi historians[1] much assistance in interpreting the dark ages of Sind. Purveyors of fiction, however, they may furnish despite themselves corroboration of the extraneous record.

From sources outside Sind there is not a little evidence testifying to something like an overlordship within the limits of the valley. The Hindu record of Gujarat, which records a long-contested war between the Solanki princes of Anhilawada and a

[1] Recorded account of the Sumrahs is hopelessly confused. The *Tuhfat-ul-Kiram* complains of the discordant accounts available; the *Tarikh-i-Ma'asumi* writes a short account of the Sumrahs because it knows of no existing account. The *Ain-i-Akbari* gives 36 Sumrah chiefs, rulers of a dynasty lasting 500 years. Ferishta makes the dynasty last 100 years. The *Muntakhib Tawarikh* gives 19 chiefs and a rule from A.D. 1053 to 1400. The *Tuhfat-ul-Kiram* alludes to the existence of more than the twelve rulers it details, and assigns them a rule of 505 years, ending in A.D. 1351. The *Tarikh-i-Tahiri* gives dates for the dynasty A.D. 1300 to 1439, whilst the *Tarikh-i-Ma'asumi* makes the Sumrah independent rule begin in 1320. The *Ain-i-Akbari* makes them follow the *Tamin-i-Ansari*; the *Tuhfat-ul-Kiram* makes them pay tribute for 200 years to Ghaznivide and Ghori emperors and elect their own leader in 1320; the *Muntakhib Tawarikh* gives them a leader in A.D. 1053.

ruler of Sind, seems to indicate the existence of a powerful and imperial sovereign in Sind. At one time we are told therein that the territory of the Sind raja extended to the sea; at another that the Sind raja had conquered the ruler of Sivasana and many another lord of fort and island. The legendary account, too, of the diversion of the Indus by Bhim, in order to circumvent the bulwark of the Sind raja, predicates an invasion of upper Sind, and the corresponding extension of the Sind sovereignty into the north of the valley. Over a period of two hundred years, from the middle of the tenth to that of the twelfth century, there is thus ground for believing in an approach to consolidated rule in Sind.[1] It is precisely within this period that other evidence points to the power of Mansura and to the strength of the Karmatian heresy. Before its disappearance Mansura had become a hotbed of revolt, political and sectarian, against the Ghaznivide rule. The Sultan Mahmud, on his return from the sack of Somnath in 1026, turned aside to oust the heretic ruler of Mansura, and carry still further the work he had begun at Multan and Uchch of exterminating heresy; Mansura figures again a few years later as the objective in his flight of Ahmed-i-Nial Tigin, a feudatory of Lahore who had rebelled against Sultan Masud.

In A.D. 1032 we hear of a Sumrah chief, Rajah Pal, to whom an appeal is made to bring back to the fold of the Karmatian heresy backsliders therefrom, and in particular the turncoat ruler of Multan. Apparently, therefore, in the eleventh century Mansura was the centre of the Karmatian heresy and the political capital of the Sumrahs,[1] who wielded some kind of overlordship over the other rulers of Sind.

It remains now to consider the leading features and political factors of the following century. At the end of that

[1] In the reign of Mularaja (A.D. 961-96) the Sind ruler supports the Abhira ruler of Sorath and the King of Cutch against the Solanki. Bhim I (A.D. 1022-64) invades Sind and defeats Hammak, King of Sind (*vide Dvaiasharaya* of Hemachandra).

The *Kirtikamundi* also mentions the binding of the lord of Sindhu, and a Dohad inscription of 1140 speaks to the destruction of Sindhuraja by Siddharaja. Sind record is entirely innocent of reference to this struggle of two centuries.

Legendary story often corroborates the surmise drawn from the limited record of history. A legend of Moghulbin and the martyrdom of the saintly Bhim speaks of a Sumrah chief ruling Cutch, Gujarat, Surat, Kach Mekran, Multan and Bakhar; the immigrant settlers of Kathiawar have among them many traditions of vassalage to the Sumrahs.

century Bakhar has appeared, symptom of a divergence between the south and north of Sind, which henceforth becomes a permanent factor in determining its history. First and indisputable evidence of its existence is in 1228, when Nasiruddin Kabajah was invested in its fort, but it had by that time acquired a reputation throughout India for power, wealth and impregnability, and a town had grown near its walls. Its first appearance is as a stronghold of orthodoxy, for the brief reign of Nasiruddin Kabajah (1203-1228) is the reply of orthodoxy to a heresy that had made empty the throne of Delhi, and Nasiruddin declares himself independent when Sultan Muizzuddin is assassinated by a Karmatian heretic.

This appearance of Bakhar implies a shifting of the political centres of the valley, and it is clear that it synchronises with the disappearance of Mansura, and that this in turn is accompanied by the rise of a power in the delta which becomes a thorn in the side of the rulers of Delhi. For it is at the end of the twelfth century that the confusion of legendary and historical record begins that confounds the names of Tatha and Debal. It is from the days of the Sultan Muizzuddin Muhammad Sam (*circa* 1182) that, according to the *Tarikh-i-Firoz Shahi* of Shamsi Siraj Afif, Tatha was considered to have been a perpetual source of trouble to the Emperors of Delhi.

By the beginning of the thirteenth century, therefore, it is beyond dispute that Bakhar in the north was balanced against a power in the delta; that Mansura from its intermediary position had ceased to be a political factor, if not ceased actually to be. Simplicity at least is obtained in unravelling the intricate confusions of the dark ages of Sind by assuming that, as orthodoxy advanced in the north, based upon the impregnability of Bakhar, the heretical power that had centred upon Mansura retired into the delta, finding in Debal, Muhammad Tur and Tatha substitutes for its medial capital.

The power which in the eleventh century had established something like a suzerainty over the greater part of the valley; that had successfully kept aloft the banner of heresy, retired in the twelfth century to the delta, where it resisted all attempts to subdue it, until in the fourteenth century it fell before the Sammahs, whose historians sang its requiem.

X

THE ALEXANDRIAN TRADITION

THE ALEXANDRIAN TRADITION

A MONOCHROME print, that draws so generously upon form and simple contrast of shade for its charm, is the best representation in judicious emphasis of much that is picturesque in Sind; it is certainly, too, a fitting accompaniment to the memoirs of the last century, that present a picture of the valley extreme in its monotone and perhaps by very reason of this conveying something intangible and elusive that provokes romance. Lugubrious, however, as is their realistic analysis of the evils of the valley, they are consistent in the sweet unreasonableness with which they embrace a great enthusiasm, that colours for them with an air of mystery and romance the apparent bequests of classic days. On the one hand is Burton, in mood as innocent as Borrow of such enthusiasm; on the other is Burnes, pressing onward with buoyant zeal to see the classic Indus, outstripping his slowly moving baggage, and after days of weary travel from the wastes of the Ran riding forty miles in a day of Sindhi sun. His eager expectation that broke a night's repose is typical of the craving for romance, the ultimate contemplation of a great idea; typical, in short, of the dynamic possession that, evinced by these old memoirs, makes them so refreshing reading to-day as symptomatic of living youth.

This sudden maturing of enthusiasm for the glory that was Greece and to be traced in Sind, is in exact accord with the many meteoric revelations of Sind record, for there is no advent of its appearance before the nineteenth century, when it flashes forth in riotous and undisciplined exuberance. Faint allusions to the great Alexander there may be in Sind's early record—there is one in the familiar legend of the Alor Bund—but there is nothing to show that Sind felt any interest in the Greek invasion before the last century, and nothing to promise the pride she has lately developed in her temporary bondage to Greece. Even the outburst of legendary story in the sixteenth and seventeenth centuries did not add Alexander to the half-legendary figures of Sind history, or give an explanatory and Greek lineage to the occupied sites of the valley.

And in a similar way there is nothing in the early record of Western travel or trade in Sind to anticipate the enthusiasm with which the European invaders of later years sought for the remains of Hellas. The story of the East India Company's adventures in the valley over several centuries is innocent of recollection of the first meeting therein of West and East; even the Indus to the East India Company's factors is almost unknown by the name it acquired in classic days, nor does the valley, save as an El Dorado of possible wealth, evoke any enthusiasm in those who visited her. Traditions of the Greek connection with Sind are indeed dead; in the travel memoirs of a few who never visited the valley the names given in classic times may still be given to the map of the valley, and the delta may be described with names anachronistic by more than a millennium of years, but so far as acquaintance with the valley goes there is nothing to forecast the development of the nineteenth century.

Much is missed in reading the old memoirs of those who first entered the valley in the last century, if the vivid keenness is forgotten with which, trained in the good old way, they sought for traces of the path of Alexander. The follies of a vision that was made the more inexact by an assumption that the present geographical features of the valley had remained unchanged for two thousand years were many. There was the pleasant logic of him who found the origin of the sacred name of Hellas in that Hala range of mountains that adjoin the Kirthar heights on the border of Baluchistan, and the derivation of 'Hellenes' in the appellation of the chiefs of Hela. There were, again, the wild etymological discoveries of Pottinger—his assumption that the island of Prasiane, mentioned by Arrian as in the delta of the Indus, was the tract around Larkana in upper Sind, because the latter was called 'Chandoki',[1] to wit,

[1] 'Chandoki,' i.e. belonging to the Baluch tribe of Chandia. Besides this making of Sind the motherland of Hellas, and this confusion with the moon of a prominent Baluch tribe, Sind record has other quaint humours. Tod furnishes one or two examples. There is his description of the Indus as a streak of blue running along the edge of a hinterland of desert—this between Hyderabad and Alor—and his discovery that Sehwan and Seistan are one, and

'moonlit,' 'glistening,' or 'fertile'. There is Tod's recognition of 'islandic Bekher' in the pages of Arrian, and Cunningham's detailed tracing of Alexander's route along the Indus of to-day; there is the tribute to Tatha of descent from Patala, and to Alor of identity with the capital of Mousikanos. In short, there is no important site or feature of the valley that has not been given an inheritance from classic days that will remain a cherished possession. One may smile now at the disappointment of Postans at not finding specimens of Greek architecture at Sehwan, and at his success in tracing the fort that Alexander there built overlooking the Indus, but the tradition will die slowly that Alexander visited Sehwan; one may be astonished at Anquetil du Perron's search for a temple built by Alexander at Tatha, but Tatha still hearkens to no natural law in its attachment to the past.

The glamour of Greece has come to Sind late, but it would seem to remain. The groves of palms along the present course of the river, strangely spaced as they are by the accident of chance, are in fond credence the product of date stones thrown away by the encamped armies of the Greeks; the well wheels of Sind moan aloud that Alexander has long ears, and the strange craft of the river bear the fashion of boats moulded by Western art.[1]

A great enthusiasm is in the essence of religion; its greatness controls the imagination and colours the aspect of ordinary things. And maybe it is better to wander far in Sind, haunted by the glamour of ancient Greece, than to travel far in an unpoetic sobriety. The realist loses much of the spice of life by analysing its sweets, and the realities of the valley

the latter's meaning 'the abode of cold'. There is, too, the confusion of a settlement officer, who confused Siwistan (Sehwan) and Siwi (Sibi), and based his report on the one on figures he obtained from the other. Less obvious is Pottinger's interpretation of 'Larkana', i.e. the residence of the tribe of Larak, as the abode of saliva or ooze. Within the last few years one of our learned societies found it impossible to consider the discovery of Greek and Greek-inspired inscriptions by an Indian Civilian in Sind.

[1] The Indus boat is made in segments, separately framed and then joined together. The historians of the Greek invasion describe the Greeks as transporting their troops in the Indian plains in boats made in segments. In 1841 Captain Wood wrote that the Macedonians had been in the habit of completing the sides and bottoms of their boats apart at the Isthmus of Corinth, *ergo* the surmise that Sindian naval architecture had its origin in Greece. The Greek divided his smaller boats into two segments, not, like the Indus boats, into three.

are not such as naturally lie hid; one moment of sweet unreason is worth many a nicely-calculated exactitude, and the unhappy valley is no mere conjunction of heat and dust. The realist will see in the Indus a tawny river, wider than the Thames but far more muddy. In suchlike mood it was that Burton addressed his descriptions of Sind to John Bull; it was but a mood, and the spirit of the memoirs of the nineteen centuries, alien to this, is that which has handed on to the Sindhi a permanent possession of pride.

APPENDICES

APPENDIX A

Khwajah Khizr

The small island shrine of Khwajah Khizr, opposite Rorhi, is one of the most picturesque features of the river at Sakhar.

The accounts of its origin would hardly be Sindhi if not conflicting. According to one account it was the merchant Shah Hassein who, in gratitude for the assistance of Khwajah Khizr in diverting the river at Alor, built a shrine, where a torch of light fell, and settled there a married pair to be custodians of the shrine . . . ancestors, of course, of those who are now custodians of the shrine. Another account makes a shepherd, Baji, whose hut was where now stands the town of Rorhi, see at night a bright flame burning in the distance. Thinking travellers had lit a fire, he first sends his wife to get a light, but as fast as she pursues the light it recedes further. Thinking his wife was afraid the shepherd then himself goes, but the light still proves as elusive as before; so, filled with awe, he erects a shrine and becomes a devotee, and the river encircles the shrine he has erected.

To-day, whilst Muhammadan worshippers worship the *Koran*, Hindu pilgrims worship a light, which is kept burning night and day. When new fruit comes to the bazaar both throw a first fruit into the river as an offering; every evening women mix rice and sugar, and with flowers and fruit throw them into the river, along the banks of which they kindle lamps. Every Friday and last day of the moon in each month is sacred to the god of the waters, and on these days the Hindu meat-eater will eat fish only as being the fruit of the water. On the birth and marriage of sons rafts are floated down the river, bearing lights, a medium through which the love-sick maiden, too, can divine the course of her love.

Legend says that the Pir dived into the water and came up at Udero Lal in the Hyderabad district; his followers wear red coverings marked with the emblem of a hand and a fish. Khizr is popularly supposed to mean 'dolphin'.

The shoals of palla, or river salmon, ascend the river as far as the shrine, and are said to do so on a pilgrimage to the shrine, on attaining which they swim round, following the strictest of court etiquette, as they never present their tails to the hallowed abode of the saint until they are well round the island and back again.

There are many parallels to this dominion over the waters and control over storms by a patron saint. Cf. Pir Badar, Zinda Ghazi, Ghazi Miyan, the Panch Pir of Bengal . . . and it is probable that such saints are the transformation of old animistic spirits, perpetuating an ancient Nature worship of daimonia and tutelary spirits. In 'Gleanings from the Si-yu-ki', Art. xii, *J.R. As. Soc.*, xvi, 1884, Professor Beal dwells upon the Buddhist myths that seem to be incorporated in the story of El Khedr and their similar appearance in the Arthurian legends.

The Muhammadans say that Al Khedr found the fountain of life, and drinking thereof became immortal. Cf. *Koran*, Sura xviii, and the inscription on a drinking cup of the emperor Jahangir:

> 'Let the water of life be in his cup,
> So that it may be the water of
> Khizr, life-prolonging.'

Al Khedr is credited with flying round and round the world, a chapel arising wherever he appears. He is Phineas, whose soul passed into Elias and thence into the sacred rider, St. George. At Sakhar he is the Zinda Pir or living Pir.

APPENDIX B

DARYAPANTHIS

The worshippers of the King-river have an account of the birth of Uderolal in this wise. At the beginning of the eleventh century, when Marakh was ruler of Tatha, the Hindus were persecuted by the Muhammadans. The king desired a single religion for the whole of Sind. The panchayat obtained a respite of three days, and went to the bank of the river at Tatha and offered prayers for three days, at the close of which they heard a voice from the river crying, 'After eight days I shall be born at Nasrapur and my name shall be Uderolal'. After this time Uderolal was born. The babe was a remarkable one ; after a few moments it became a youth, then a black-bearded man, and again an old white-haired man. The king's vazir summoned him to Tatha, but instead of following the vazir he suddenly appeared from the river at Tatha at the head of an armed regiment, which, however, he commanded to return to the river.

He was then brought before the king, who tried to obtain his help to convert the Hindus, but he declined, saying that Turks and Hindus were alike to God. Then at his vazir's advice the king tried to arrest Uderolal, but no one could catch him as he changed his form now to air, now to water.

Then the king proceeded with the forcible conversion of the Hindus, whereon Uderolal commanded fire to destroy the town ; the king repented, begged pardon, and Uderolal insisted on perfect freedom of worship for all.

At the age of twelve Uderolal ordered his cousin to found the sect of Daryâpanthis, and gave him a lamp, sword, and, among other things, a jar of sacrificial water. The Muhammadans were brought to adopt the same religion by a miracle. Uderolal wished to purchase the land of a Muhammadan, who wished first to take the advice of his wife, and left Uderolal in the full blaze of the sun, but returned to find that a large tree had grown up to shade Uderolal. The Muhammadan gave the land gratis to Uderolal, who, after striking the ground and bringing forth diamonds and rubies for the Muhammadan, was swallowed up by the ground, he and his horse.

The king then decided to build a mausoleum on the spot, and, guided by a voice they heard at night, the king built a mausoleum and the Hindus another place adjoining, in which lamps should be kept.

The two places exist still. Muhammadans do not go to the lamp building, but Hindus go to both. The lamps are lit and maintained by the Hindus. The Muhammadans only collect the offerings. This is the tomb where the lamps, five in all, are lit at nightfall; in the other building lamps are kept burning day and night. The holy tree exists, and no common person is allowed to touch it. Its seeds are a cure for sonlessness.

A fair is held on the first day of Chaitr, to which followers come from Sind, Cutch and the Punjab.

After his disappearance at Jhai-jo-goth Uderolal appeared at Bakhar from the rock. Here, too, a great fair is held for forty days, before which the Hindus lock the doors of the holy place of Zinda Pir and allow only a caretaker to enter the cave, in which is maintained a light. Even the caretaker is prescribed in his movements, and must approach the shrine swimming on an earthen pot and with his eyes bandaged. The Daryâpanthis maintain their caste by exogamy. They have three sections: (*a*) the Somâi; (*b*) the Budhâis centring on Sehwan; (*c*) the Ghorâis around Mehar, who neigh like a horse when approaching a village of their own section.

N.B.—This legend of the birth of Uderolal makes Tatha the capital of Sind in the eleventh century (*cf.* foot-note on p. 50).

APPENDIX C

The Indus Boat

It matters not whether you confine yourself to the great river itself with its broad and open reaches, whether you follow the meanderings of its branching canals into their most intimate silence, or whether you leave both river and canal and wander over the quiet lakes, or 'dhands', of the Indus valley. The boat of the valley is everywhere the same in general form. In miniature it is not unlike the punt of Western streams and reed-choked waters, the craft of philosophic ease and contented idling; in larger scale it is an uncouth barbarism, with a great redemption in its towering yard and lateen sail. The fashion of its building is wondrous. Its sides and bottom are first separately completed, and then brought together like the sides of a box; where the bow and stern are to rise the planks are lubricated with a mixture that, combined with applied force, gives them a curve upwards. And the completed boat appears a caricature of river art, picturesque and quaint with her rising ends and great rudder, or oar in place of rudder. She is a thing of strange curves and stranger lines; a fretwork of inconsequent timbers, and, as horses and cattle or lumbering camels leap over her low gunwale on to that unprotected bottom, one wonders at the fate that gives her a normal life of seven years. Yet the caricature has its truths, and in the quaintest of her barbarisms is an unexpected response to the needs of the river and the dangers of its ever-shifting channels. And when the river traffic was a matter of greater import than it is now, and the improvement of its ancient craft was considered, it is remarkable that little alteration of her eccentricities could be proposed.

Within recent times a great change has taken place in the rig of the Indus boat, and the influence of the Arab dhow from the harbour of Karachi has added a pleasing feature to the river. For there is now no more familiar object on the river than the great wing-like sails that in their delicate curves are so alien to the crude lines and dimensions of the hulls they overshadow. They break with an atmosphere of Oriental romance and Eastern light into the dull river scenes of drab monotony; they suggest a joy of motion that is sadly belied by the ungainly forms beneath them, and manifest a conscious controlled art inconsistent with empiric creation. They are the one unchanging feature in the valley of constant aspiration, drawing the eye upwards where almost all else lies low and earth-bound in humility. Never was stranger mating than this union of the sail of inland seas with the hull of mud-stained river, or this captivation of airy freedom by ungainly impotence.

In the nineteenth century an oblong sail accentuated the heavy impression of inert immobility conveyed by the irresponsive mass below. Pottinger, Wood, Postans and Burton describe this ancient sail, but thirty years after Burton wrote is mention of the lateen sail. From the days of his sovereignty in the valley the Arab has bequeathed few legacies to Sind; it is his fortune that centuries later he has given the valley one of its most attractive insignia.

APPENDIX D

Mathelo

One of the oldest sites in Sind. Rai Sihasi II remitted assessment on condition that his subjects built for him kilas at Arore, Uchch, Siwistan, Mathelo, Mau and Suri. (A.D. 630.)

A verse of nine lines is still repeated by local residents giving the history of the town:

'The first brick of Mathelo was laid by Jam Parian, some masonry was done by Rai Gharano. (A.D. 495.) For some days there were Thahims, after which came the turn of Warhiaries. The kot was ready in 900 years. After this Raja Nind ruled there. After Raja Nand Mathelo came into the hands of the Mahars. Dharejahs married a woman to Mahars, in return for which Mahars gave them Mathelo, after which Mahars did not live in Mathelo.'

Mathelo is so called because it is on high ground. The ending is applied to other villages, e.g. Ghotki is called Sahibanjanji Loi.

Mathelo, like Alor, was a fortified place of importance even in the time of the Emperor Akbar. It still had then its own Governor.

APPENDIX E

Moghulbin

Major Raverty writes that after the annexation of the Tatha territory the Khan-i-Khanan Mirza Abd-ur-Rahim wished to see the ocean before he returned to the court at Agra, that he set out from Tatha with this purpose, and proceeding about thirty miles obtained the sight he wanted. The place from which he obtained this view, he continues, is called Moghulbin in consequence to this day, *bin* being the Persian for 'seeing', 'view', 'sight'. The story is a romantic one, on the model of the story of Alexander going out to sea and of Hadrian in A.D. 116 after the capture of Babylon. The late Dr. Vincent Smith repeats the story. The *Tarikh-i-Ma'asumi*, however, says the Khan-i-Khanan went to Lahribandar, where he gazed upon the sea.

In early maps of the nineteenth century the place is written Mugribin, Muggurbhee, which are nearer approximations to the present spelling than is Major Raverty's interpretation. The correct writing is Mughar Bhain, مغر بهين. Local tradition gives about A.D. 1311 as the date of its foundation. It attributes the name to two martyrs of battle, Bhain and his son, Mughar. In Jati taluka men still carry the name of Bhaindino, and in the shrines at Moghulbin Mughar and Bhain have their separate tombs. The present Khalifa claims to be of the same caste as Pir Bhain, and the Thaims are numerous in the taluka, who still have connection with Lakhpat, whence Bhain traditionally came.

MAPS

Maps to illustrate conceptions of the Indus Delta and the Ran of Cutch

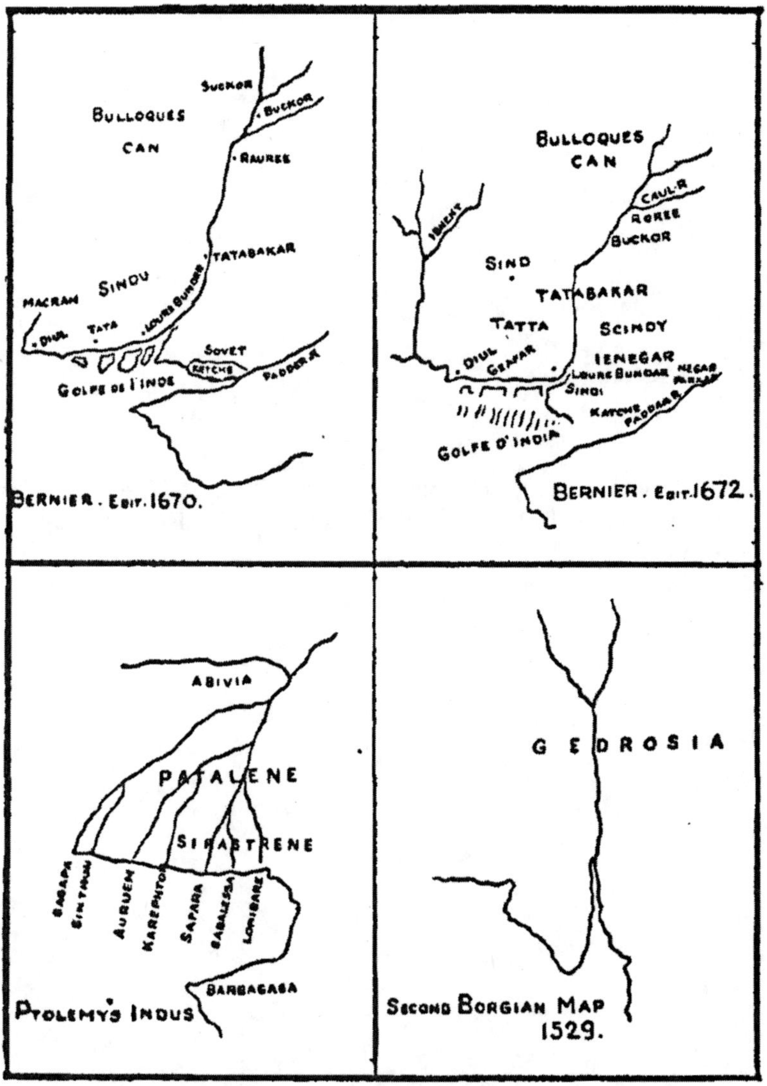

(*a*) FROM BERNIER (1670). (*b*) FROM BERNIER (1672). (*c*) PTOLEMY'S MAP OF THE INDUS. (*d*) THE SECOND BORGIAN MAP OF 1529.

The maps on p. 111, save the first, illustrate the separation of the river of Debal from the Indus. *Vide* also the maps of Bernier.

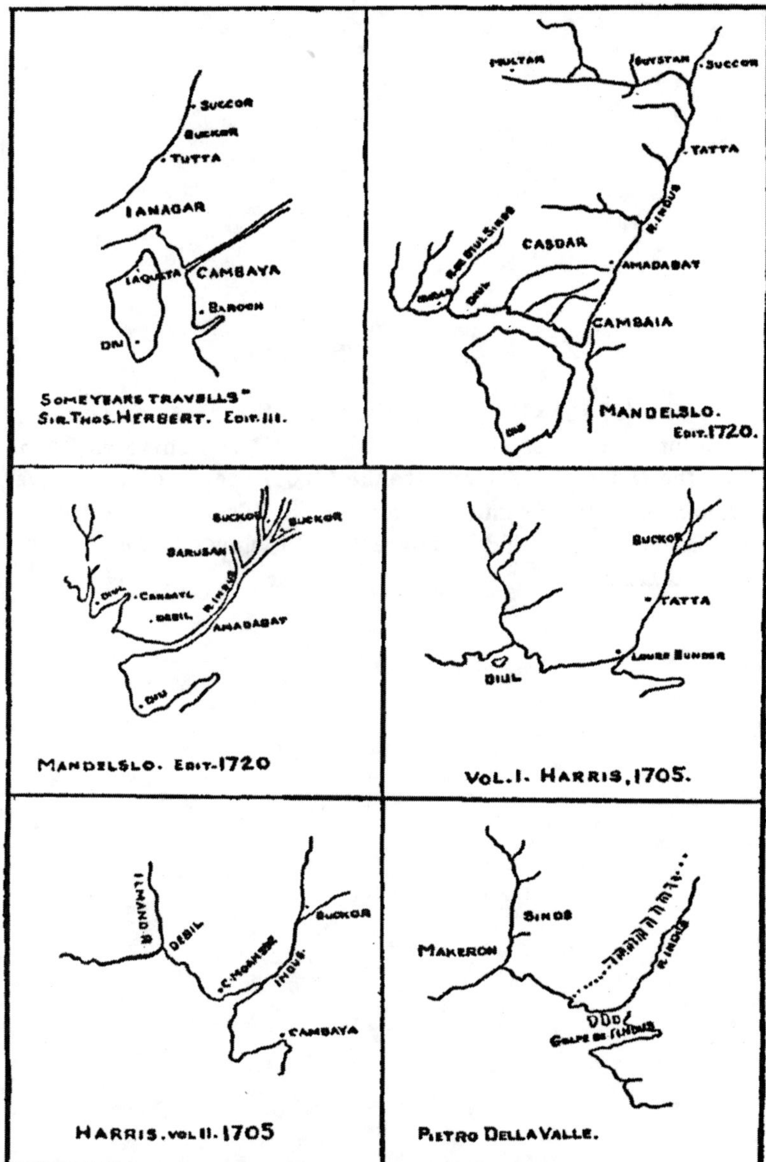

(*a*) Sir Thomas Herbert's Map. (*b*) From Mandelslo (1720). (*c*) Another Map of Mandelslo's (1720). (*d*) Harris' Map (1705). (*e*) Harris (vol. II), (1705). (*f*) Pietro Della Valle's Map.

Map (*b*) shows the 'Damiadee'. Sir T. Herbert (1626) mentions this river along with others of the Punjab as falling into the Indus. Joseph Salbanke (1609) speaks of the 'River Damiadee' running into the river of 'Synde', close by the city of 'Buckar'. It would be interesting to know whether this was the old Hakra.

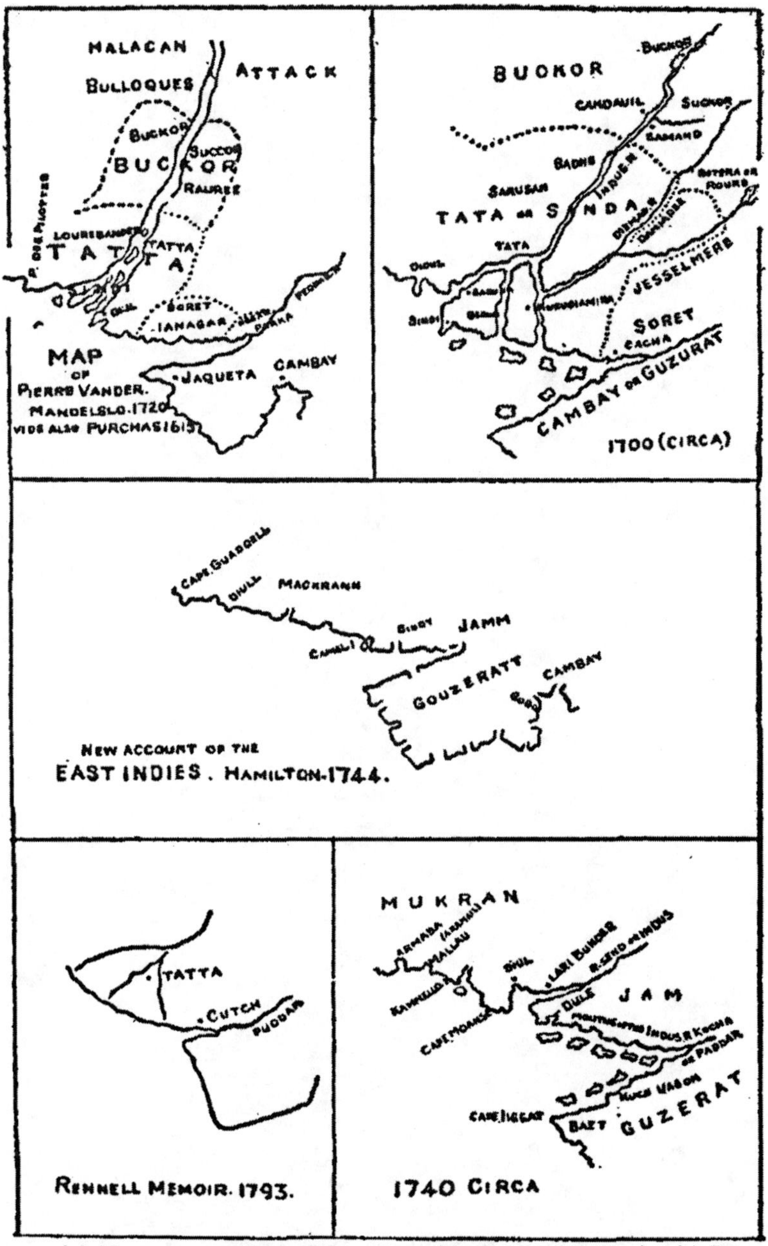

(*a*) Mandelslo's Map (1720). (*b*) A Map of 1700 (circa). (*c*) From Hamilton's East Indies (1744). (*d*) From Rennell's Memoir (1793). (*e*) A Map of 1740 (circa).